JUDGING NONVIOLENCE

JUDGING NONVIOLENCE

The Dispute Between
Realists and Idealists

MANFRED B. STEGER

ROUTLEDGE
NEW YORK & LONDON

Published in 2003 by
Routledge
29 West 35th Street
New York, NY 10001
www.routledge-ny.com

Published in Great Britain by
Routledge
11 New Fetter Lane
London EC4P 4EE
www.routledge.co.uk

Routledge is an imprint of the Taylor & Francis Group.
Printed in the United States of America on acid-free paper.

10 9 8 7 6 5 4 3 2 1

Library of Congress Cataloging-in-Publication Data

Steger, Manfred B., 1961–
    Judging nonviolence : the dispute between realists and idealists / Manfred B. Steger.
        p. cm.
    Includes bibliographical references and index.
        ISBN 0-415-93396-X (alk. paper) — ISBN 0-415-93397-8 (pbk. : alk. paper)
    1. Nonviolence. 2. Nonviolence—Philosophy. I. Title.
    HM1281.S746 2003
        303.6'1—dc21   2003009381

For my students

We think that to be able to tell the truth, as difficult as it might be, to be able to face the powerful without violence, to face them as we do, gives us strength, a different kind of power, not their kind.

The Mothers of the Plaza de Mayo

CONTENTS

LIST OF ILLUSTRATIONS

LIST OF BOXES

PREFACE AND ACKNOWLEDGMENTS

Is it possible to engage in power politics and yet remain nonviolent in theory and practice? Can political ends be achieved by nonviolent means? Is Martin Luther King, Jr.'s dream of a nonviolent society applicable to the "real world"? Can a violent aggressor be repelled nonviolently?

These questions have been at the center of undergraduate classes on the politics of nonviolence that I have been teaching at two American universities for almost a decade. Although some of my students remained skeptical about the possibility of fully reconciling nonviolent principles and political power, the vast majority of them nonetheless conceded at the end of the semester that nonviolence constitutes a far more potent political method than they had originally thought. Nearly unanimous in their opinion that nonviolent forms of political struggle are not being given fair consideration in a society in which violence is habitually sanitized and normalized, my students urged me to write an accessible college text based on our highly successful class format of "putting nonviolence on trial." After several years of being too busy to write such a text, I have made doing so a priority.

In addition to attesting to my students' persistence, this book is also a testimony to my own desire to challenge the dominant ideology of violence. Expressed in cold numbers, the social and environmental impacts of violence are truly frightening. Researchers have calculated that war-related killings in the twentieth century exceeded 105 million people, including 62 million civilian victims. Still, there is little indication that we have learned the bloody lessons of the past. Let us consider contemporary American society. Today, U.S. citizens own a total of 70 million rifles, 65 million handguns, 49 million shotguns, and 8 million other long guns. More than 15,000 Americans are murdered each year. Every day in the United States four women are murdered by a male partner.

Each year, 6 million women are beaten in their homes. Each year, as many as 6.9 million American children may by physically abused, depending on the definition used. Total homicides in the United States since World War II are estimated to be at least 750,000, thus exceeding the 650,000 total battle deaths in all of America's major wars. The prison population in this country has exploded to 1.8 million, including almost 4,000 convicts who await execution.

This goes to show how the pervasiveness of our culture of violence makes reliance on force a normal occurrence. Add to this culture of violence the widespread and easy availability of arms and you get an explosive recipe. To be sure, the obsession with violence is not an exclusively American phenomenon. Yet many studies have shown that Americans are far more accepting of violence than citizens of other nations. Rates of violence are much higher in the United States than in any other industrialized nation. For example, there is a dramatic contrast between levels of violence in Canada and the United States, two countries that share a long common border and many similar values and cultural traits. For more than half a century, levels of violence as measured by homicide rates have consistently been four times higher in the United States than in Canada.

From the day they are old enough to sit in front of a television set, American youngsters are fed a steady stream of media images and sound bites that often depict violence as heroic and inevitable. Video games and popular music frequently glamorize violence. Jeff Bleich, executive director of the National Campaign Against Youth Violence, has long argued that violence constitutes a central pillar of the American belief system. We encourage boys—and increasingly girls—to believe that in order to become honorable persons, they must demonstrate that they are willing to use violence. Our enthusiasm for guns, our glorification of war and the military, our choice of superheroes, our appetite for violent sports games, and our use of belligerent language reflect the myriad ways in which we put violence at the center of our collective identity. And yet, violence is a financial drain on the resources of a nation. Conservative calculations show that the U.S. nuclear weapons program alone cost taxpayers almost $6 trillion during the last five decades.

One reason why nonviolence is so easily dismissed in public discourse seems to be obvious: a serious consideration of nonviolent strategies might create an alternative vantage point from which the alleged normality of violence could be challenged. This widespread reluctance to afford the subject of nonviolence a more prominent place in our public discourse and educational programs points to the remarkable power of social forces with vested economic and political interests in protecting the business of violence—be it violence-glorifying entertainment, war, or the global arms trade. Often hiding their commercial interests behind the language of "security" and "necessity," these forces habitually downplay the feasibility of nonviolent politics. Instead, they present violence as a universal urge or set of unalterable biological behaviors sewn into the very fabric of human nature that get played out on the allegedly anarchic stage of international politics. The nonviolence movements of the twentieth century are dismissed as either grand moral experiments that ultimately failed or rare exceptions that merely confirm the (violent) rule.

Drawing on a variety of political, cultural, and philosophical insights, this textbook provides students and general readers with vital information about nonviolence in theory and practice while encouraging them to evaluate critically the arguments for and against nonviolence. Assuming the role of jurors in a simulated trial in which nonviolence must prove its effectiveness, readers will be asked to listen attentively and impartially to the first-person testimonies given by expert witnesses for the prosecution (the realists) and for the defense (the idealists). Jurors will weigh direct and circumstantial evidence; rethink their preconceived opinions; follow up on possible questions for cross-examination; explore further readings; consider exhibits such as illustrations, films, and web sites; and, finally, find nonviolence guilty or not guilty as charged by the realists.

The reason for putting nonviolence (rather than violence) on trial is simple. I am not interested in merely singing the praises of nonviolence. To take seriously the claims of the tradition of Gandhi and Martin Luther King means to go beyond the delivery of morally edifying sermons. Both realist and idealist perspectives on nonviolence rely on myths and narratives that contain a mixture of strong and weak arguments. To endorse nonviolence without exposing its possible shortcomings would do a serious disservice to the complexity and seriousness of our subject.

Much to their credit, most students intuitively dislike one-sided presentations. The juror format adopted in this book commits students to the ideals of fairness, impartiality, and rationality, thus allowing them to consider the potential of the nonviolent method in politics. Just as democracy cannot survive without formal deliberation exercised by an educated citizenry, intellectual progress depends on people's willingness to reflect critically on dominant norms and ideas—in this case, the reigning ideology of violence.

It is always a pleasant duty to record my debts of gratitude. The research and writing of this book would not have been possible without the support of many individuals and institutions.

First and foremost, I am grateful for the numerous suggestions and helpful comments made by more than two hundred undergraduate and graduate students at Whitman College and Illinois State University. I admire their intellectual energy and passionate engagement.

Countless interactions with academic colleagues helped me to revise and hone my own ideas on the subject of (non)violence and pacifism. I want to thank, in particular, Ursula Baatz, Lawrence Besserman, Robert Bobilin, Steve Bronner, Franz Broswimmer, Terrell Carver, Lane Crothers, Thomas Eimermann, Kathy Ferguson, Alan Gilbert, Manfred Henningsen, Jeffrey Isaac, Timothy Kaufman-Osborn, Jamal Nassar, John Kautsky, Ramdas Lamb, Peter Manicas, Khalil Marrar, Ron McCarthy, Glenn Paige, Carlos Parodi, Sherri Replogle, Michael J. Shapiro, Phyllis Turnbull, and Amentahru Wahlrab.

I greatly appreciate the support of my two indefatigable graduate assistants, Ken Panfilio and Ryan Canney. Their boundless energy provided a big boost to this project. The organization of this book has also benefited from Cynthia Weber's exemplary textbook, *International Relations Theory: A Critical Introduction* (Routledge, 2001). Professor Weber's book is a model for an approach to challenging students' preconceptions of the political world without being preachy or boring.

Illinois State University's steady support of my work and the professional travels related to this book included a summer research grant and a one-semester sabbatical leave. I am grateful to Kay Stults, graphic designer at ISU, for helping to design the maps. Eldon Wegner, chair of the Department of Sociology at the University of Hawai'i, generously provided me with ample office space during the 2002–3 academic year.

I want to thank Karen Wolny, publishing director at Routledge, for believing in this book. Karen's keen editorial eye and her catching enthusiasm never fail to impress me. Finally, as always, my deepest sentiments of gratitude go out to Perle, my soul mate and best friend.

Manfred B. Steger
Bloomington, May 2003

CHAPTER ONE

INTRODUCTION
Nonviolence on Trial

Nonviolence Accused: The Terrorist Attacks of September 11, 2001

Realism and Idealism

The Three Charges

Instructions to the Jurors

Clarification: What Is Meant by "Nonviolence"?

Suggestions for Further Reading and Thinking

Nonviolence Accused: The Terrorist Attacks of September 11, 2001

When al-Qaeda terrorists crashed three hijacked American commercial airliners into New York's World Trade Center and the Pentagon in Washington, D.C., people around the world were shocked by the scale and ferocity of these attacks. Opinion polls taken in the United States and Europe in the aftermath of these events showed that citizens particularly disapproved of violence directed against unsuspecting civilians. Indeed, many people felt that no political end could ever justify the exercise of terrorist violence.

And yet, many opinion polls revealed that large majorities on both sides of the Atlantic endorsed the idea of responding to the attacks with a massive dose of retaliatory military violence. In the United States, about 90 percent of the population supported a full-scale "war on terrorism"—

even if such a military campaign lasted for several years and cost tax-payers hundreds of billions of dollars. Invoking a nation's right to self-defense, most commentators in the U.S. media concurred with President George W. Bush's argument that the only "rational" way of dealing with such terrorist "evildoers" was to "smoke them out of their holes" and destroy their capacity to launch further attacks.

Opinion polls conducted throughout 2002 showed that only a small minority—about 5 to 10 percent of Americans—disagreed. Some of these dissenters argued that the terrorist attacks of September 11 should be seen not as an act of war against the United States but as a heinous crime against humanity. Expressing a qualified commitment to nonviolence, they favored an internationally coordinated response that would include the imposition of economic and political sanctions against nations harboring terrorists, the creation of an international police force to apprehend those responsible for the 9/11 attacks, and criminal trials of al-Qaeda terrorists before an international court of law. Only very few dissenters expressed an unqualified commitment to nonviolence by categorically opposing all forms of retaliatory military violence. They insisted that exchanges of lethal force would only pull the world further down a descending spiral of terrorist strikes and counterstrikes, ultimately setting the stage for a new generation of terrorists.

The overwhelming media reaction to these minority views was anger, scorn, and derision. Many commentators referred to the members of the dissenting minority as irrelevant "pacifists" blinded by their political naïveté and suffering from a lack of patriotism. These accusations were repeated even more stridently when, in the aftermath of 9/11, European and North American peace activists organized sizable demonstrations against the expanding war on terrorism.

Claiming that nonviolent strategies won't work against hard-edged terrorists, mainstream media pundits presented the war on terrorism as an act of purest logic: kill or be killed. In fact, some commentators went even further, insisting that the pacifists' refusal to endorse a military campaign amounted to a hypocritical, immoral, and treacherous position. Hypocritical because pacifists enjoy the liberties and democratic arrangements that someone else's engagement in violence has created in the first place. Immoral because nonviolence does not constitute a realistic alternative strategy in a situation where one's country has been attacked by ruthless killers. Treacherous because a commitment to non-

BOX 1.1
WHAT IS PACIFISM?

The term "pacifism" refers to a system of norms, values, and beliefs that reflect opposition to war. Although pacifists usually support nonviolent forms of conflict resolution, it is important to remember that the concepts of pacifism and nonviolence are related but not necessarily the same. A pacifist is a person who holds that war is wrong and therefore opposes the violence of war. Whether a pacifist opposes all forms of violence may differ from person to person. Some pacifists make an "unqualified" or "absolute" commitment to nonviolence, arguing that violence is wrong under any conceivable circumstances. "Pragmatic" or "situational" pacifists explicitly renounce the violence of war, but are willing to consider milder forms of violence. Constituting a minority in most modern societies, pacifists are often derided as "traitors," "cowards," or "dreamers" by the majority who believe that, if employed legitimately, war and other forms of large-scale violence constitute a proper and necessary means of resolving political conflicts.

violence not only undermines the virtues of patriotism and military resolve but also encourages terrorists to strike again.

Although similar accusations have been leveled against pacifists and nonviolent activists for a long time, they have acquired new salience in the wake of the al-Qaeda attacks. Indeed, such a resolute rejection of nonviolence as both a philosophy and a method of political engagement is part and parcel of the dominant political ideology of realism.

Realism and Idealism

As noted above, the critics of nonviolence argue that those who enter the arena of politics had better adopt a "realistic" outlook on the world—one that sees the arena of power politics as moved primarily by self-interest and lust for power. From a realist perspective, ideals, morals, and concern for the common good are but rhetorical rationales for expedient, self-interested action. How do realists justify these assumptions?

First and foremost, they claim that human nature is fundamentally aggressive and, therefore, flawed and sinful. Hence, humans are prone

---

BOX 1.2
NONVIOLENCE ACCUSED: TWO NEWSPAPER EXCERPTS
The American pacifists wish the Americans to not fight. If the Americans do not fight, the terrorists will attack America again. And now we know such attacks can kill many thousands of Americans. The American pacifists, therefore, are on the side of future mass murderers of Americans. They are objectively pro-terrorist. . . . A war has been declared; you are either on one side or another. You are either for doing what is necessary to capture and kill those who control and fund and harbor the terrorists, or you are for not doing this. If you are for not doing this, you are for allowing the terrorists to continue the attacks on America. You are saying, in fact: I believe that it is better to allow more Americans—perhaps a great many more—to be murdered than to capture and kill the murderers. That is the pacifists' position, and it is evil.

Michael Kelly, *The Washington Post*, September 26, 2001

Pacifist demonstrations may work against the occasional repressive government or program, especially if the media are handy, but not against terrorism. In fact, terrorists love pacifists. . . . The pacifist who demonstrates against his own country's military policies is exercising a right that was created with blood and born of violence. Not random violence, like the terrorist act, but violence resorted to out of necessity. That single fact is what makes the pacifist's complaint so unpalatable.

Kathleen Parker, *Chicago Tribune*, November 28, 2001

---

to violent conflict. Greed, hatred, and aggression are the chief motivating forces of human behavior, realists say. They believe that fear of overwhelming violence plays an important restraining role in politics. After all, they insist, the only reliable way of keeping people's destructive impulses in line is to create a governing authority whose capacity to unleash violence is greater than that of any other group in society.

Second, realists believe that the overriding interest of humans is biological survival. Ultimately, the inherent need to prolong one's life overrides less tangible spiritual values and moral concerns. The most obvious strategy to ensure biological survival is to increase political power by building a strong state. The existence of a powerful state is essential for people who desire to secure their possessions and acquire new ones. Hence, the interests of the state predominate over all other interests and values.

Third, realists assume that we live in a world of scarcity. Hence, politics is a zero-sum game: there are winners and losers. Violent battles over those limited resources are an inevitable part of the human experience.

Overall, then, realists believe that war and other forms of violent behavior are sewn into the very fabric of human nature. In their view, the idealist desire to rid the world of violence is not only a utopian fantasy but also a dangerous notion whose realization would foster more aggressive behavior. Realists have no problem with violence as such; the pivotal question is who wields it and to what end. They insist that violence must be made "legitimate," that is, put into the hands of the lawful representatives of the state solely for the purpose of maintaining domestic social order and repelling foreign aggression.

Pacifists and other adherents to nonviolence subscribe to an idealist model of politics. In their opinion, ideals, morals, and concern for the common good play a major role in politics. Self-interest and the lust for power are contingent social factors rooted in bad types of political organizations and poor forms of social communication. How do idealists justify their assumptions?

First and foremost, they argue that human nature is basically good. Given the fact that humans are malleable social animals, however, they

---

BOX 1.3
WHAT IS IDEOLOGY?

An ideology is a system of widely shared ideas, patterned beliefs, and guiding values accepted as fact by some group in society. Ideologies organize the tremendous complexity of the human experience into fairly simple and understandable images and slogans. Rooted in the power interests of particular groups and classes, ideologies always contain a political dimension, for they are ultimately about the many ways in which power is exercised, justified, and altered in society.

---

are also susceptible to selfish behavior and other forms of corruption. Still, their violent impulses are not unalterable elements of their biological makeup but the result of bad forms of socialization. For example, some idealists argue that the capitalist economic system fosters competitiveness, selfishness, and materialism. Others make our political system of nation-states responsible for creating pernicious divisions among people. Idealists believe that love, not fear, constitutes the chief motivating force of human behavior. In their view, a profound reform of existing social institutions toward greater cooperation and better communication would drastically reduce violence within and among societies.

Second, idealists believe that people's overriding interest is not merely biological survival but happiness and spiritual fulfillment. The best strategy to reach these objectives is to allow citizens equal access to political and economic power. A democratic system based on equality and individual liberty makes it easier for all citizens to cultivate high moral standards and secure ample material resources.

Third, idealists assume that we live in a world of plenty. Scarcity is not the natural state of affairs but a human-induced condition that reflects the workings of exploitative social arrangements. Once these arrangements have been reformed, violent struggles over limited resources will become a distant chapter in human history.

Overall, then, idealists believe that war and other forms of violent behavior are rooted in society, not in human nature. In their view, the desire to rid the world of violence is not a utopian fantasy but a feasible

---

BOX 1.4
REALISM IN INTERNATIONAL POLITICS

The term "realism" is associated with an anarchic model of international politics. "Anarchy" denotes the absence of a single global political authority—such as a world government—that could impose binding rules on nation-states. Given this inescapable condition of anarchy in the international sphere, sovereign nation-states must compete with each other in order to increase their power and ensure their survival. Thus, the interests of the state predominate over all other interests and values. Realists consider war and other forms of large-scale violence unavoidable features of political life.

BOX 1.5
IDEALISM IN INTERNATIONAL POLITICS
The term "idealism" is associated with a cooperative, interdependent model of international politics. Idealists believe that politics could be reorganized around global political institutions, such as a world government, that would impose binding rules on nation-states. Ceding much of their power to these global institutions, countries would no longer be bound to a relentless dynamic of national competition. In this way, war and other forms of large-scale violence could be eliminated from political life.

---

program whose realization would make our planet a better place. Idealists have a problem with violence as such; the question of who wields it and to what end is less important. Insisting that violence is not a necessary means for the maintenance of social order, idealists are instead guided by the ideals of peace and international cooperation.

The exploration and evaluation of the main arguments emerging from these two opposing perspectives on nonviolence—realism and idealism—are at the center of this book. The moment has arrived when you, the critical reader, are asked to assume a more active role in discerning and evaluating the claims made by spokespersons for each side.

The Three Charges

For the remainder of this book, let us assume that you have been selected to serve as a juror in a trial of nonviolence. The jury system has had a long tradition in Europe. It is believed that Norman invaders brought it to England in the early Middle Ages. There are two types of juries: the grand jury of accusation and the petit jury of trial. The former usually consists of twelve to twenty-three randomly chosen persons who have been given authority to issue criminal charges and indictments. The latter usually consists of twelve randomly chosen persons who, after carefully evaluating pertinent evidence, must reach a verdict of guilty or not guilty. The main task of each petit juror is to decide whether the testimony of a witness is trustworthy and to weigh the relative value of conflicting evidence in the case. Thus, jurors are asked to make a sincere commitment to consider the facts in an impartial and unbiased manner in order to uncover the truth.

Because jurors are charged with evaluating the facts rather than interpreting the law, they are not required to have any special legal training. Indeed, the best jurors are frequently ordinary persons who possess little knowledge of legal matters. What makes somebody an excellent juror is his or her willingness to listen carefully to the testimonies of the witnesses and to let go of preconceived opinions and prejudices.

To be a juror in our simulated trial of nonviolence, you do not have to know anything about either the law or international politics. The entire process has been greatly simplified to help you evaluate the quality of the testimonies given by the expert witnesses for the prosecution and the defense. Please bear in mind that while the testimonies of the expert witnesses are ficticious, they nonetheless convey the thinkers' central views and positions on the subject. Both the plaintiff (legitimate violence) and the defendant (nonviolence) are not persons of flesh and blood but more or less coherent philosophical positions and an associated set of political behaviors. The main arguments of each side will become more apparent as the trial unfolds. The prosecution (realists) will let their three expert witnesses make their case against nonviolence directly to you; the defense (idealists) will follow the same procedure.

At the end of each chapter, you will find a list of questions that an experienced trial lawyer might pose to the expert witnesses during cross-examination. Please apply these questions to the testimony you have heard and ascertain possible responses by following up on the suggestions for further reading and thinking. After analyzing and evaluating additional evidence drawn from recent nonviolent social movements, you must find nonviolence guilty or not guilty as charged. You will receive more detailed jury instructions in the next section.

For the moment, then, let us assume that a grand jury has affirmed an indictment of nonviolence prepared by the realist prosecution. The indictment contains the following three charges.

The Three Charges Against Nonviolence

1. *Charge*: Nonviolence is contrary to human nature.
   Specification of charge: Since human nature is inherently flawed and sinful, people engage in violence. Moreover, our instinct for self-

preservation compels us to compete for scarce resources, thus making violence inevitable in human affairs, particularly in power politics.

2. *Charge*: Nonviolence does not work in the real world.
   Specification of charge: The proof of the impracticality of nonviolence is that its proponents do not achieve their desired political and social goals.

3. *Charge*: Nonviolence does not provide adequate security.
   Specification of charge: The refusal to employ defensive violence makes people far more vulnerable to their violent neighbors and enemies. To opt for nonviolence means to neglect one's social responsibility and risk the safety of one's community.

Instructions to the Jurors

The faithful performance of your jury duties is vital to the administration of justice. The law applicable to this case is contained in these instructions and it is your duty to follow them. Rather than selecting one instruction and disregarding others, you must consider these instructions as a whole.

- Nonviolence, the defendant in this case, is presumed innocent until proved guilty beyond any reasonable doubt. The defendant is entitled to the same fair and unprejudiced treatment as an individual would be under like circumstances, and you should decide the case with the same impartiality that you would use in deciding a case between individuals.

- The evidence you are to consider consists of the testimonies of expert witnesses, evidence drawn from social movements and science, and exhibits (such as illustrations, films, and web sites) offered and received. In determining whether any proposition has been proved, you should consider all of the evidence bearing on the question, without regard to which party produced it.

- There are two types of evidence that you may properly use in deciding whether the defendant is guilty or not guilty. One type of evidence is called *direct evidence*. Direct evidence is where witnesses testify to what they saw, heard, or observed. In other words, when witnesses testify about what is known to them of their own knowledge by virtue of their own senses—what they have seen, felt, touched, or heard—that is called direct evidence.

Circumstantial evidence is evidence that tends to support a disputed fact by means of other facts.

Here is a simple example of circumstantial evidence. Assume that when you came into the classroom this morning the sun was shining and it was a nice day. Assume that the classroom blinds were drawn and you could not look outside. As you were sitting there, someone walked in with an umbrella that was dripping wet. Somebody else then walked in with a raincoat that also was dripping wet. Now, you cannot look outside of the classroom and you cannot see whether it is raining. So you have no direct evidence of that fact. But, on the combination of facts that you were asked you to assume, it would be reasonable and logical for you to conclude that it was now raining. That is all there is to circumstantial evidence. You infer on the basis of reason and experience and common sense from an established fact the existence or the nonexistence of some other fact.

- Circumstantial evidence is of no less value than direct evidence. It is a general rule that the law makes no distinction between direct and circumstantial evidence but simply *requires that before convicting a defendant, the jury must be satisfied of the defendant's guilt beyond a reasonable doubt from all of the evidence in the case.*

- An inference is not a suspicion or a guess. Concluding that a disputed fact exists on the basis of another fact you know exists is a reasoned, logical decision. There are times when different inferences may be drawn from facts, whether proved by direct or circumstantial evidence. The prosecution asks you to draw one set of inferences, while the defense asks you to draw another. It is for you and you alone to decide what inferences you will draw.

- You are the sole judges of the facts. It is your duty to determine the facts, and to determine them from the evidence produced in open court. You should consider all of the evidence or lack of evidence in reaching your verdict. Neither sympathy nor prejudice should influence you. Your verdict must be based on evidence, and not on speculation, guess, or conjecture.

- You are the sole judges of the credibility of the witnesses, and of the weight to be given to the testimony of each of them. In determining the credit to be given to any of the witnesses, you may take into account their opportunity to observe; their memory; any interest, bias, or prejudice they may have; and the reasonableness of their testimony, considered in the light of all the evidence in the case.

- Moreover, in evaluating credibility of the witnesses, you should also take into account any evidence that the witness who testified may benefit in some way from the outcome of this case. Such an interest in the outcome creates a motive to testify falsely and may sway the witness to testify in a way that advances his or her own interests. Therefore, if you find that any witness whose testimony you are considering may have an interest in the outcome of this trial, you should bear that factor in mind when evaluating the credibility of his or her testimony and accept it with great circumspection.

- All witnesses in this trial of nonviolence have been qualified as experts. Expert witnesses are permitted by the judge to express an opinion on those matters about which they have special knowledge, skill, experience, and training. Such testimony is presented to you on the theory that someone who is experienced and knowledgeable in the field can assist you in understanding the evidence or in reaching an independent decision on the facts. In weighing this "opinion testimony," you may consider the expert witness's qualifications, his or her opinions, the reasons for testifying, as well as all of the other considerations that ordinarily apply when you are deciding whether to believe a witness's testimony. You should not, however, substitute the experts' opinion testimony for your own reason, judgment, and common sense. The determination of the facts in this case rests solely with you.

- If you find from your consideration of all the evidence that some or all charges against the defendant, nonviolence, have been proved, then your verdict should be against the defendant on those counts. If, on the other hand, you find from your consideration of all the evidence that the charges have not been proved, then your verdict should be for the defendant.

Clarification: What Is Meant by "Nonviolence"?

It seems that we are now sufficiently prepared to commence the trial by calling on the first expert witness for the defense. Except for one important thing: What exactly is meant by the term "nonviolence"? In a trial of a real person, you would be able to make visual contact with the accused, observe his or her behavior, and learn about his or her background. Our case is more difficult because our defendant is not a person but a philosophical position with an associated set of political behaviors. To be sure, some details about the "background" of nonviolence will come to light in the testimonies of the expert witnesses and the evidence drawn from social movements.

Various scholars, legal experts, and social activists have invoked the concept of nonviolence in different, often confusing, ways. Let us bring some conceptual clarity to the term by first considering its etymological roots. The word "violence" comes from the Latin verb *violare*. It comprises a range of meanings, including "to force," "to injure," "to dishonor," and "to violate." For the purpose of this trial, we are interested in the significance of these meanings solely as they relate to human interactions and not in the more broad applicability of the term "violence" to occurrences in the natural world such as storms, earthquakes, or the predatory behavior of animals. As humans, we engage in violence when we use force to injure or dishonor somebody purposely. This element of intention implies that, in addition to its obvious physical aspect, violence also contains a psychological dimension. Examples of psychological violence include threats, insults, and the "ill will" that usually precedes or accompanies physical acts of violence and causes other people mental anguish.

Some scholars, such as the Norwegian peace researcher Johan Galtung, prefer a wider definition of violence that extends beyond its physical and psychological dimensions. Defining violence as an "avoidable insult to basic human needs," Galtung emphasizes the hidden, or "structural," dimension of violence caused by political or economic structures of exploitation and inequality. One obvious example of structural violence would be the persistence of poverty—a phenomenon exacerbated by the failure of rich countries to offer more economic assistance to less developed nations. Since citizens of wealthy countries in the Northern Hemisphere tend to benefit from the workings of these exploitative social and economic systems, they are implicated in the persistence of structural violence, even if they don't purposely inflict physical or emotional pain on people in the global South.

Galtung's broad definition of violence has the advantage of allowing us to consider important structural aspects. However, it also com-

---

BOX 1.6
NONVIOLENCE DEFINED
Nonviolence is a philosophical position and an associated set of political actions of those who refrain from the intentional infliction of physical and psychological injury on persons.

---

plicates the picture by downplaying the crucial element of personal intention. For the purpose of this book, it makes sense to adopt a more restricted definition: *violence is the intentional infliction of physical or psychological injury on a person or persons.* Conversely, nonviolence is the absence of intentional infliction of physical or psychological injury on persons. However, such a definition in purely negative terms seems to make nonviolence look meek and passive. This is especially misleading in a situation where the *political* potential of nonviolence is under scrutiny. Indeed, in a political context, both violence and nonviolence are characterized not by the absence of political activity but by the presence of certain kinds of political actions. To reiterate, nonviolence is not merely a philosophical position but also a set of associated political behaviors. Thus, in your role as jurors, you are not to automatically assume that nonviolence is tantamount to passivity, indifference, or the absence of political action. Rather you should note that it includes activities such as letter writing, picketing, demonstrating, and, in some cases, engaging in acts of civil disobedience.

Suggestions for Further Reading and Thinking

Topic 1. The Jury Trial Process

Those of you who are interested in learning more about the jury trial process will find a plethora of relevant books and stimulating audiovisual materials available. Especially in Anglo-American countries, there has always been a fascination with real-life courtroom dramas. Recent examples include the highly publicized trials of the football celebrity O. J. Simpson, Microsoft Corporation, and Arthur Andersen Accounting Partnership. As a consumer of popular culture, you can choose among several regular TV shows set in courtrooms that include the highly successful series *Judge Judy* and *The People's Court*. Unfortunately, these shows often seek to boost ratings by crudely putting human emotions on display and trivializing important social issues. Still, these programs also attest to the popularity of the judicial system in our culture.

Suggested Reading

Nathan Aaseng. *The O. J. Simpson Trial: What It Shows Us About Our Legal System*. New York: Walker, 1996.

Jeffrey Abramson. *We, the Jury: The Jury System and the Ideal of Democracy*. Cambridge, Mass.: Harvard University Press, 2000.

D. Graham Burnett. *A Trial by Jury*. New York: Knopf, 2001.

Cornelius P. Callahan. *The Search for Truth: An Introduction to the Jury Trial Process*. Chicago: Sextant Press, 1997.

Recommended Visual Materials

Twelve Angry Men. Dir. Sidney Lumet. 1957. Feature film.

Useful Web Sites

www.jefferson-center.org/citizen_jury.htm

www.abanet.org/mediafajury.html

www.crfc.org/americanjury

Topic 2. Nonviolence in Theory and Practice

As we struggle to meet the new political and moral challenges in our post-9/11 world, the question of violence and its alternatives will only gain in importance. Hence, it is essential for you to familiarize yourself with some of the pertinent discussions in the social sciences and humanities. You might want to visit your local library and check out some of the suggested books below. Don't be intimidated; though some of them are fairly substantial collections of essays, you don't have to read them from cover to cover. Just pick out some essays that pique your interest. Broadening your knowledge of the various academic approaches to our subject will improve your ability to evaluate the testimonies of our expert witnesses.

Suggested Reading

David P. Barash, ed. *Approaches to Peace: A Reader in Peace Studies*. New York: Oxford University Press, 2000.

Robert L. Holmes, ed. *Nonviolence in Theory and Practice*. Belmont, Calif.: Wadsworth, 1990.

Michael N. Nagler. *Is There No Other Way? The Search for a Nonviolent Future*. Berkeley, Calif.: Berkeley Hills Books, 2001.

Manfred B. Steger and Nancy Lind, eds. *Violence and Its Alternatives: An Interdisciplinary Reader*. New York: St. Martin's Press, 1999.

Jennifer Turpin and Lester Kurtz, eds. *The Web of Violence: From Interpersonal to Global*. Urbana: University of Illinois Press, 1997.

Recommended Visual Materials

Alternatives to Violence. Prod. William Whitlock. WTL Productions, 1982. Video.

Useful Web Sites

www.nonviolence.org
www.globalnonviolence.org
www.forusa.org
www.rcnv.org

PART I

The Expert Witnesses for the Prosecution

CHAPTER TWO

NICCOLO MACHIAVELLI
Renaissance War Realism

Historical Background and Credentials of the Witness

Machiavelli's Testimony

Questions for Cross-examination

Suggestions for Further Reading and Thinking

Figure 2.1 Niccolo Machiavelli, 1469–1527. Courtesy of Corbis.

Historical Background and Credentials of the Witness

Niccolo Machiavelli was born in the Italian city-state of Florence at the height of the historical period known as the Renaissance. Roughly the years spanning 1400 to 1600, this era marks the beginning of modernity. The term Renaissance means, literally, "rebirth" and signifies the rebirth of classical literature and the arts in Europe after almost a thousand years of cultural stagnation. As artists and intellectuals developed a great interest in the ancient civilizations of Greece and Rome, they sought to imitate the grandiose style of the masters of antiquity. Originating in the city-states of the Italian peninsula and spreading to the rest of Europe, the Renaissance movement carried forward a spirit of enthusiastic inquiry into the disciplines of rhetoric, architecture, the visual arts, literature, philosophy, and politics. Famous Italian "Renaissance men" such as

Marsilio Ficino (1433–99) and Pico della Mirandola (1469–1533) proudly considered themselves "humanists" who projected in their literary works the new image of humans as free individuals and creators of their own destinies. Thus humanists challenged medieval church doctrine that assigned people a fixed station in life.

Machiavelli, too, was an ardent humanist who showed far more interest in the temporal world of artistic beauty and political power than in the eternal world of the beyond. Educated to cherish people's capability to fashion their own lives according to secular ideals, young Niccolo came to admire the military leaders of antiquity whose strategic brilliance and courage on the battlefield brought honor, glory, and prosperity to their respective homelands. In the fifteenth century, Italy was not yet a unified nation-state. A political map of Renaissance Italy shows a patchwork of hundreds of small and mid-size political entities; some were principalities ruled by aristocrats or bishops while others were republics dominated by a handful of wealthy families. The most powerful of these statelets were Venice, Milan, the Kingdom of Naples, the Papal States in Central Italy, and Florence. Engaged in perpetual warfare, each state sought to expand its territory and establish itself as the dominant power on the Italian peninsula.

During Machiavelli's youth, Florence was dominated by the powerful Medici family. Starting out as successful bankers and merchants, the Medici eventually seized political power and ruled the city as the grand dukes of Tuscany. In 1494, the Medici lost political influence as a result of shifting military alliances caused by the invasion of the Italian peninsula by French and Spanish troops. Eventually they were expelled by wealthy Florentine families, who set up a republic under the able leadership of Piero Soderini (1452–1522). Noticing Machiavelli's considerable political talents, Soderini appointed him secretary and second chancellor of the republic. His diplomatic duties required Machiavelli to visit many Italian city-states. He also traveled to the court of the powerful French king and spent some time at the splendid Viennese residence of the Holy Roman Emperor Maximilian I.

In 1505, Soderini ordered Machiavelli to organize a citizens' army. As the new chancellor of the militia, the Renaissance equivalent of today's secretary of defense, Machiavelli worked hard to recruit and train ordinary Florentine citizens in the art of war. His troops, however, were a bitter disappointment, losing several crucial battles against a mercenary army financed by the former aristocratic masters of Florence. In 1512, the Medici triumphantly returned to the city and restored their authoritarian rule. After only 18 years, the republican experiment in Florence had ended in military defeat.

Dismissed from office, imprisoned, tortured, and exiled to the outskirts of Florence, Machiavelli spent the rest of his life in relative isolation and obscurity. With much free time on his hands, he embarked on an ambitious literary career. His chief works include the brilliant comedy *La Mandragola* (The Mandrake) (1518), the political tracts *Discourses on the First Ten Books of Livy* (1519) and *The Art of War* (1520), and the historical treatise *Florentine Histories* (1525). However, it was a political booklet titled *The Prince* (1513) that brought lasting fame to its author. Hoping that this short text might attract the attention of the restored rulers of Florence and thereby help revive his political career, Machiavelli dedicated it to Lorenzo de Medici.

The book offers advice to potential and actual princes on how to acquire new territories and rule in a bold and decisive manner. As the founder of modern realism, Machiavelli was not particularly concerned about adhering to existing standards of morality. Instead, he counseled princes to pay attention to the "real world" of politics with its unavoidable conflicts, wars, and conspiracies. In his view, a well-equipped military constituted the only solid foundation on which to build a stable order that benefited rulers and subjects alike. Ironically, Machiavelli died shortly after the restoration of the Florentine republic in 1527—at the very moment when his political career was about to be resuscitated.

Overall, then, Machiavelli's impeccable credentials make him a strong expert witness for the realist prosecution. He possesses extensive knowledge of diplomatic affairs, military strategy, historical events, and political philosophy. Moreover, his personal experience with warfare and the struggle for political power add a valuable pragmatic dimension to his professional résumé. Having traveled extensively in Europe, he offers an important cross-cultural perspective on the role of (non)violence in politics. Thus, without further ado, let us call to the witness stand His Excellency Niccolo Machiavelli, ex-chancellor of the Florentine republic. Jurors, please bear in mind that while this testimony is not an actual speech given by Machiavelli, it nonetheless conveys his central positions and views on the subject.

Machiavelli's Testimony

Esteemed jurors,

I am pleased to be called before you as an expert witness for the prosecution. In my view, the three charges against nonviolence are solid and entirely justified. My opinion on this matter is based on long years of professional experience as a Florentine diplomat, military leader, eminent historian, and political philosopher. Please allow me to elaborate on my reasons for supporting the indictment. Let us start with the first charge: *Nonviolence is contrary to human nature. Since human nature is inherently flawed and sinful, people engage in violence. Moreover, our instinct for self-preservation compels us to compete for scarce resources, thus making violence inevitable in human affairs, particularly in power politics.*

I totally agree with this statement. Violence *is* inevitable in human affairs because human nature is violent. Unfortunately, there is not much to be done about it; we're just born this way. I wish I could give you better news, but I can't. That's the truth. Why do I say this? Because I'm a practical person who pays attention to things as they really are. I do not allow myself to get sidetracked by things as they ought to be. Believe me, during my long years of public service, I had the opportunity to gain deep insight into the workings of human nature. I've observed people in different cultural settings and political circumstances. I've seen over and over again what happens in politics and how people behave toward each other in their frantic scramble for power. I have been an eyewitness to assassination, murder, betrayal, lying, cheating, and deception. You name the evil deed—I've seen it. Not only once or twice but many times. Not just in Italy but in all of Europe. Human nature is inherently flawed, regardless of our biological and cultural differences. Listen to the following example.

Orphaned at a very young age, Oliverotto was raised by his uncle, Giovanni Fogliani, an influential citizen of the small city-state of Fermo. Giovanni made sure that his nephew received a privileged officer's commission in the army that would virtually ensure him a brilliant military career. Showing great prowess and intelligence, the young soldier soon advanced to the rank of general. Determined to seize power for himself, Oliverotto came up with a duplicitous scheme. Writing to his uncle that he longed to present himself to his fellow citizens as a loyal champion of Fermo, he asked Giovanni to convince the other civic leaders to allow him to enter the city with his 100–soldier honor escort. He also urged his uncle to invite the leading citizens of Fermo to a festive banquet at his expense. Proud of his nephew's military achievements and pleased by his apparent generosity, Giovanni readily agreed to make the requested preparations. At the banquet, Oliverotto gave a secret sign to his soldiers, who charged out of their hiding places and killed his uncle and the other guests of honor. After the slaughter, Oliverotto took over the palace and set up a new government, over which he declared himself prince. Within a few days, he had his remaining enemies executed. He further strengthened his position by founding new civil and military institutions.

I'm sure you know of similar military takeovers that happened in your time. This bears out my contention that the basic makeup of human nature never changes. Most likely you disapprove of Oliverotto's actions, thinking that he was an ungrateful wretch who repaid his uncle's kindness with the most heinous crime imaginable. I'm asking you to reconsider. Oliverotto merely did what human nature dictates in the struggle for political power: dominate or be dominated. In fact, by following his natural political instincts without allowing himself to be held hostage to conventional rules of morality, he not only established himself as Fermo's new ruler but also made his city-state formidable to all neighboring states. In short, the citizens of Fermo reaped the benefits of Oliverotto's audacious actions as they prospered under his leadership. This shows that the interests of the state should always predominate over all other interests and moral values.

If my conclusions sound harsh and crude to you, please accept my sincere apologies. I don't want to offend your moral sensibilities. At the same time, however, I won't mar my testimony with fancy words or empty etiquette. I'm here to tell you the truth as I see it, and that's what I'm going to do. It may be brutal, but at least you'll be confronted with the raw facts of human nature. Who can deny that humans have always behaved violently in the pursuit of political power? Starting with Cain and Abel, there have always been murders, wars, rapes, and mutilations. Please don't get me wrong, I'm *not* saying that violence is *all* there is to politics. Responding strictly to the wording of charge number 1, I'm arguing that violence is inevitable—and indeed necessary—in human affairs, particularly in power politics. In fact, the most distinguished mark of the master politician is his ability to elevate the exercise of violence to a science and thus learn to use cruelty well.

Moreover, a capable politician is also an expert in using a broad range of means to achieve his political goals. Given our capacity for rational calculation, we humans need not resort to brute force all the time. Sometimes, we can use less violent strategies to achieve our objectives. At times, it's enough to threaten our enemies. At other times, we lie or distort things a little. On still other occasions, we are left with no choice but to go to war. Whatever our choice might be, to assume that humans can pursue political power without ever resorting to violence would be as ridiculous as to say that lions can remain kings of the jungle without ever killing a single antelope. It's a mistake to think that we humans can simply transform our violent animal natures. Rather than being ashamed of our beastly impulses, we ought to realize that we can learn many useful things from our relatives in the animal kingdom. A successful politician must be like a fox in order to recognize traps, and like a lion to frighten off other aggressors. If humans were inherently good, there would be no need to give this testimony; but because men are wretched creatures, my expert opinion carries much empirical weight.

Let us now turn to the second charge: *Nonviolence does not work in the real world. The proof of the impracticality of nonviolence is that its proponents do not achieve their desired political and social goals.*

History is full of examples that show conclusively that nonviolence does not work in the real world. Remember, I'm talking about the real world, not those imagined worlds dreamed up by political thinkers in their ivory towers, which have never in truth been known to exist. In the real world people get killed, promises are broken, and dreams of love and understanding are shattered. The fact is that a politician who wants to be nonviolent necessarily comes to grief among so many who remain violent. If you want to maintain your power you must learn how not to be good, and use that knowledge, or refrain from using it, as necessity requires.

Here is my favorite example of the impracticality of nonviolence. Girolamo Savonarola (1452–98) was a Dominican friar who condemned

---

BOX 2.1
MACHIAVELLI ON HUMAN NATURE
One can make this generalization about men: they are ungrateful, fickle, liars, and deceivers; they shun danger and are greedy for profit. The bond of love is one which men, wretched creatures that they are, break when it is to their advantage to do so.

BOX 2.2

MACHIAVELLI ON SELF-PRESERVATION

There is such a difference between the way we really live and the way we ought to live that the person who neglects what is actually done for what should be done learns the way to self-destruction rather than self-preservation.

---

from his pulpit the vices of worldly power and moral laxity. His fiery preaching style brought him considerable political influence in Florence as large crowds flocked to his church to listen to his prophecies. The chief architect of the city's 1494 republican constitution, Savonarola soon emerged as the most powerful leader of Florence. Thinking that his oratory skills were enough to keep him in power, he made a costly mistake: he failed to build up an army loyal to his command. When his influence over the masses gradually waned, he had no effective means available to keep backsliders in line. His enemies immediately seized upon this golden opportunity. Excommunicated by the Pope Alexander VI, Savonarola was imprisoned, tortured, and executed within a few weeks.

Now let us consider an instructive counterexample. Philopoemon, the leader of the Achaeans, has been justifiably praised by historians for having never thought of anything else except the condition of his army and innovative military strategies, also in peacetime. Every day, when he rode out into the country with his commanding officers, he would stop frequently and ask them, "Suppose there were enemies up on those hills, and you were here with your army, who would have an advantage? How would you attack them? If they tried to get away, how would you cut them off?" As a result of these constant reflections on war and battle, Philopoemon prepared himself for almost any military emergency. Consequently, his enemies feared him. Although they coveted his power, they never dared challenge his leadership.

Nonviolent political leaders are bound to fall short of their desired goals, because it is unreasonable to expect that an armed person will ever obey one who has no means of violence at his disposal. Formidable weapons represent a great advantage in the scramble for scarce resources, thus serving the ultimate goal of self-preservation much better than thin appeals to moral principles.

The second reason why nonviolent prophets won't reach their political goals relates to public opinion. Experience teaches us that, in the long run, the masses won't stick with nonviolent prophets. As borne out in the case of Savonarola, people may be enchanted with pious sermons for a while. In the end, however, they'll despise nonviolent politicians for being too effeminate, cowardly, and unrealistic. If a political leader wants to be successful, he must, at all cost, avoid being hated or despised by the people. Remember that hatred is not the same as fear. Strengthened by the threat of punishment, fear is an effective sentiment that must be mobilized by a capable leader in order to keep people in line. But it is always disadvantageous for a person in charge to be despised, since low public esteem invariably emboldens conspirators and military challengers.

There is simply no comparison between the social prestige enjoyed by the man who is prepared to employ arms and that of a person who refuses to exercise violence. Don't forget that, throughout history, all known societies and cultures have celebrated war and violent combat in some form. Military heroes are held in high esteem, and public holidays and ceremonies remind the people of their invaluable service to their homeland. It is utterly unreasonable to expect that such positive public sentiments toward necessary forms of violence will ever disappear.

Finally, let me say a few words related to charge number 3: *Nonviolence does not provide adequate security. The refusal to employ defensive violence makes people far more vulnerable to their violent neighbors and enemies. To opt for nonviolence means to neglect one's social responsibility and risk the safety of one's community.*

Much of what I've said with regard to the first two counts finds its logical extension in this third charge. Imagine what would happen if you were entrusted with safeguarding the well-being of your community and

---

BOX 2.3
MACHIAVELLI ON THE IMPORTANCE OF ARMS
The main foundations of every state, new states as well as ancient and composite ones, are good laws and good arms. One cannot possess good laws without good arms. This means that where there are good arms, good laws inevitably follow.

you decided to become nonviolent. There you are, the great nonviolent leader, sitting in your country and announcing, "I'll be nonviolent because I want to be good. I want to be meek and humble. After all, Jesus told us that this is the way we're supposed to live. I will love my enemies. I won't even threaten them. I will turn the other cheek." Just give it a week or two. Your neighbors will hear about it. What'll be their response? Most likely, they'll be rubbing their hands with joy, saying, "Oh great, there's a nonviolent leader. Let's incorporate his nonviolent territory into our violent empire." What are you going to do? Will you greet the invaders on the border? Perhaps you'll tell them, "Hey, you, you're very bad. You shouldn't be doing this. You're not obeying God's commandments." It is preposterous to think that your appeals to the conscience of your enemies will change their actions.

Contemplate the consequences of your nonviolent posture on the well-being of your fellow citizens. By relying on a philosophy of nonviolence, you're committing yourself to passivity—a posture that virtually assures that your people will suffer. They will get killed, raped, and injured by the thousands. I understand that there are some people who really like to suffer. They're called masochists. Sure, I strongly recommend nonviolence to masochists. But those of you who are not masochists had better consider the intelligent use of defensive violence. After all, by choosing nonviolence, you're actually opening the door to more violence. On the other hand, if you maintain an effective army you will reduce potential and actual violence. In some circumstances, the best defense is offense. Rather than waiting for an attack, you might want to take the initiative. Your power grows with your expanding territory, making it less and less likely that you'll be the target of external or internal aggression. Moreover, you'll bring stability and prosperity to your state. People won't starve or get killed. They will be most grateful to you for giving them a good life. As long as you keep the masses happy, your hold on power will remain secure.

Believe me, dear jurors, I would rather live in a nonviolent world. I would rather deal with human beings who have no ulterior motives or selfish desires. But the real world just happens to be an imperfect place. In politics, the name of the game is power and violence. Different forms of violence, of course, as the situation requires. There is no single formula that fits all circumstances. As a politician you have to be flexible, weigh your options, and make your choice. If you want to succeed in the struggle for power, you have to become an expert in the administration of violence.

Esteemed jurors, please reflect carefully on my testimony. I have no doubt that reason will lead you to the right conclusions. It is my expert opinion that nonviolence should be found guilty on all three charges.

Questions for Cross-examination

1. Machiavelli paints a dark picture of human nature. If it is true that people are liars and deceivers, can Machiavelli himself be trusted to tell the truth?
2. Much of Machiavelli's testimony draws on his experience as a military leader who organized the Florentine army. Do his military defeats undermine the pragmatic value of his advice?
3. In the "real world" of power politics, Machiavelli's schemes and actions landed him in prison and permanent exile. Is his testimony, therefore, an example of an imagined world dreamed up by a failed politician? If so, does this failure turn his realism of violence into an idealization of violence?
4. Much of Machiavelli's testimony is based on historical examples. Is history always a reliable predictor of what might be possible in the future?
5. Do humans always put self-preservation above moral principles? If so, how do we explain, for example, the behavior of religious martyrs who die rather than abandon their spiritual commitments?
6. If human nature is inherently flawed and sinful, why do humans in

---

BOX 2.4
MACHIAVELLI ON SECURITY: WAR REALISM
A political leader should have no other object, no other thought, and no other subject of study than war, its rules and disciplines. The art of war is all that is expected of a capable ruler. The fastest way to lose a state and ruin its inhabitants is to neglect the art of war; the quickest way to win a state and bring honor and prosperity to its inhabitants is to master the art of war.

most societies create value structures that put love and goodwill above selfishness and deceit?

7. Machiavelli claims that public opinion favors leaders who exercise violence. Are there examples of nonviolent figures who have been held in high esteem by many people over a long period of time?

8. Machiavelli links power to violence. Is it conceivable that one could be nonviolent and yet powerful? Does power always work through violence?

9. Does a violent defense of the community guarantee its survival? Does a violent defense make the community's survival more likely in all circumstances?

10. Why is it impossible to develop nonviolent forms of defense that might be just as effective as violent forms? How does Machiavelli know?

Suggestions for Further Reading and Thinking

Topic 1. Did Machiavelli Really Mean What He Wrote in The Prince?

There has been much speculation in the academic community as to whether Machiavelli actually believed in the principles and strategies laid out in *The Prince*. There are a number of reasons for such lingering doubts. First, Machiavelli's political career unfolded in the Florentine republic. Indeed, his most substantial political treatise, *Discourses on the First Ten Books of Livy*, contains a spirited defense of republican government against the authoritarian rule of princes. Hence, some scholars have argued that *The Prince* is an opportunistic tract that reflects not Machiavelli's true political views but his willingness to write whatever it took to find employment with the Medici. Other commentators have suggested that *The Prince* should be read as Machiavelli's ultimate revenge against his torturers. By portraying Renaissance princes for "what they really were"—greedy, deceitful, and cruel—he revealed to his audience the hypocrisy and immorality of aristocratic rule. Finally, some scholars believe that *The Prince* is not a work of serious political theory but a shallow patriotic polemic aimed at inspiring a young military leader to take on the difficult task of liberating Italy from the French and Spanish invaders. We know that Machiavelli greatly admired the bold military campaigns of Cesare Borgia, the duke of Valentino and son of Pope Alexander VI. After Cesare Borgia died prematurely in 1507 without accomplishing the unification of Italy, Machiavelli might well have taken it upon himself to arouse the patriotic passions of a new generation of political leaders.

Most likely we'll never know for certain whether Machiavelli really meant what he wrote in *The Prince*. As jurors, your task is straightforward: take his testimony at face value and subject it to critical scrutiny. The readings and visual materials below will help you to study his arguments more closely. Start by reading the Norton edition of *The Prince*. It contains valuable interpretations by prominent scholars. Next read *Discourses* and compare its main ideas with those put forward in *The Prince*. Finally, tackle a short, well-written biography, such as *Niccolo's Smile*, that places Machiavelli's thought within its proper historical framework.

Suggested Reading

Niccolo Machiavelli. *The Prince*. Critical Norton Edition, 2nd ed. New York: W. W. Norton, 1992.

Niccolo Machiavelli. *Discourses on the First Ten Books of Livy*. Trans. Harvey C. Mansfield, Jr., and Nathan Tarcov. Chicago: University of Chicago Press, 1998.

Harvey C. Mansfield, Jr. *Machiavelli's Virtue*. Chicago: University of Chicago Press, 1998.

Maurizio Viroli. *Niccolo's Smile: A Biography of Machiavelli*. New York: Farrar Straus & Giroux, 2002.

Recommended Visual Materials

Machiavelli on Political Power. Dir. Bernard Wilets. Chicago: Encyclopedia Britannica Educational Corporation, 1982. Videocassette.

Useful Web Sites

www.the-prince-by-machiavelli.com
www.historyguide.org/intellect/machiavelli.html

Topic 2. The Influence of Machiavelli's War Realism on Contemporary Leaders

There is no doubt that over the centuries Machiavelli's writings have influenced many important political leaders. Three totalitarian dictators of the twentieth century—Adolf Hitler, Joseph Stalin, and Benito Mussolini—all claimed to have read *The Prince* and expressed great appreciation for its author's political advice. Even democratic leaders like U.S. President John F. Kennedy, U.S. Secretary of State Henry Kissinger, and French President Francois Mitterand found strong words of admiration for "the father of political realism."

Today, the term "Machiavellian" has become particularly fashionable in business circles and among fans of popular psychology. Signifying amorality, craftiness, manipulation, and killer instincts, Machiavellism is no longer a negative term in our tough world of mega-capitalism and international competition. Indeed, popular television shows like *Survivor* and *The Weakest Link* celebrate these Machiavellian qualities.

For a better understanding of Machiavelli's influence on the realist tradition in international politics, read a few chapters in Jonathan Haslam's *No Virtue like Necessity*. Some of the suggested books below recommend that contemporary leaders in politics and business imitate Machiavellian strategies and tactics. Unfortunately, the "advice" offered in this type of literature often remains rather superficial and trivial. If you prefer lighter fare, I recommend watching the videos listed below—they are entertaining and contain a lot of useful information.

Suggested Reading

Stanley Bing. *What Would Machiavelli Do? The Ends Justify the Meanness*. New York: HarperBusiness, 2000.

Jonathan Haslam. *No Virtue like Necessity: Realist Thought in International Relations since Machiavelli*. New Haven: Yale University Press, 2002.

Robert Kaplan. *Warrior Politics: Why Leadership Demands a Pagan Ethos*. New York: Random House, 2001.

Dick Morris. *The New Prince*. New York: Renaissance Books, 2000.

Harriet Rubin. *The Princessa: Machiavelli for Women*. New York: Dell, 1998.

Recommended Visual Materials

The Prince. Dir. Dale Minor. Princeton, N.J.: Films for the Humanities and Sciences, 2001. Video.

Machiavelli Today. Dir. Adrian Baenninger. New York: Insight Media, 1981. Video.

Useful Web Sites

www.emachiavelli.com

www.geocities.com/CapitolHill/Lobby/9559/bios.html

CHAPTER THREE

MAX WEBER
Modern Realism

Historical Background and Credentials
of the Witness

Weber's Testimony

Questions for Cross-examination

Suggestions for Further Reading and
Thinking

Figure 3.1 Max Weber,
1864–1920. Courtesy of
Max Weber Berufskolleg,
Düsseldorf, Germany.

Historical Background and Credentials of the Witness

Max Weber's life (1864–1920) roughly coincides with a period in modern European history that saw the meteoric rise of Germany to the position of a world power. After the Prussian army won decisive victories over Austria (1866) and France (1870), the road toward German national unification was open. Under the capable leadership of the Prussian prime minister, Prince Otto von Bismarck (1815–98), the North German confederation joined with Bavaria, Württemberg, Baden, and Hesse to create the Second German Empire, in 1871. King Wilhelm I of Prussia was crowned German emperor, and Bismarck was appointed imperial chancellor. During the following decades, the new empire enhanced its military capabilities and increased its economic productivity, but the pace of its political democratization limped far behind these developments. Defeated in World War I (1914–18), the German Empire collapsed and was succeeded by the Weimar Republic. Unfortunately, this new democratic order turned out to be but a short-lived political experiment that ended with Adolf Hitler's seizure of dictatorial powers in 1933.

Max Weber was born into an upper-middle-class family of successful Prussian industrialists and professionals. The family lived in the Prussian capital, Berlin, where Max Weber, Sr., was an important lawyer and member of the Prussian House of Deputies and the Reichstag (imperial parliament). He represented a moderately conservative political party that championed the interests of big business. By the time young Max was old enough to enter college, he had made the personal acquaintance of many powerful figures in German public life, thus acquiring a sophisticated insider's view of domestic and foreign politics. After studying law and political economy at the universities of Heidelberg and Berlin, Weber completed a year of military service. Ultimately, he completed his tour of duty as a reserve officer in the imperial army. In 1894, Weber accepted a prestigious academic position as a full professor of political economy at the University of Freiburg. Two years later he moved to the University of Heidelberg, where he became a professor in the Department of Political Science.

Following the death of his father in 1897, Weber suffered severe episodes of depression. Despite his receiving ample medical treatment, his illness showed no sign of abating, and he became incapable of carrying out his professional duties. Forced to retire from his academic post, Weber sought to regain his health in the more favorable climate of Italy, but his condition improved only slowly. In 1904, he was finally well enough to assume the editorship of a leading academic journal dedicated to the study of capitalist development. During the next few years, Weber managed to write several important books and articles, including a sociological study titled *The Protestant Ethic and the Spirit of Capitalism*. In this famous treatise, Weber advances the thesis that ascetic norms and values rooted in Calvinist belief structures played an important role in the successful development of capitalism.

At the outbreak of World War I, Weber volunteered for military service. Owing to his relatively advanced age, he was given a noncombatant position as administrator of a military hospital. As the war wore on, Weber's nationalistic fervor cooled considerably and he became politically active in the movement to bring about a negotiated peace settlement. After the war, he briefly joined the official German peace delegation in France. For a time, Weber was under serious consideration for high political office, including secretary of the interior in the newly established Weimar Republic. However, when these political career opportunities failed to materialize, he resolved to return to academic life as professor of political economy at the University of Vienna. At the zenith of his intellectual productivity, Weber contracted pneumonia and died at the age of fifty-six.

Max Weber's writings span a period of more than a quarter of a century. His most significant political works include "The Nation-State and Economic Policy" (1895) and "The Profession and Vocation of Politics" (1919). The main arguments of these two famous essays appear in his testimony below. A staunch German nationalist with a clear preference for democratic political arrangements, Weber interpreted politics as a ceaseless struggle that pitted nation-state against nation-state. A vocal supporter of Germany's expansionist policies before World War I, he felt that his homeland's new status as a world power left the government no choice but to advance its national self-interests by any means necessary. Like his Florentine colleague four centuries before him, Weber insisted that politics was no place for the realization of lofty moral ideals. At the same time, however, he revised and adapted Machiavelli's Renaissance war realism to fit the fundamentally changed political and military context of the early twentieth century.

Weber's impressive résumé makes him a strong expert witness for the realist prosecution. Trained in virtually all disciplines of the social sciences, humanities, and legal studies, he possesses a penetrating understanding of the workings of modern society. As a reserve officer and close observer of the first global war in human history, he is familiar with the military requirements of the modern world. Weber was an active participant in the power politics of his era, and his grasp of political affairs goes beyond a purely academic perspective. In addition to traveling extensively in Europe and the United States, Weber studied the cultures and religions of Asia. Thus, he brings an important cross-cultural perspective to bear on his analysis of nonviolence. Please give your full attention to Professor Max Weber's expert testimony.

Weber's Testimony

Honored jurors,

I appreciate having been selected as an expert witness for the prosecution. My long years of experience as a distinguished academic, soldier, and participant in public affairs compel me to offer a testimony that is largely critical of the defendant. In my view, the three charges against nonviolence are substantive enough to withstand serious rational scrutiny. With your permission, I will now consider the first charge: *Nonviolence is contrary to human nature. Since human nature is inherently flawed and sinful, people engage in violence. Moreover, our instinct for self-preservation compels us to compete for scarce resources, thus making violence inevitable in human affairs, particularly in power politics.*

If you read this charge carefully, it should become rather obvious that the statement contains two central assertions. The first relates to the composition of human nature; the second addresses the manifestations of human nature in the realm of politics and society. As far as determining the essential qualities of human nature is concerned, it could be argued that a social scientist such as me might not be the appropriate authority to consult. Fair enough. At the same time, however, I ought to point out that the so-called experts on the subject—most of them eminent theologians and philosophers—have offered little proof for their speculations. In particular, they have failed to produce the sort of empirical evidence that would pass the rigorous standards of modern science.

Rather than adding to these fruitless debates, I prefer to anchor my comments on the first charge against nonviolence in one simple but irrefutable observation: *humans cannot exist without physical bodies.* Consequently, whatever we imagine "human nature" to be, it cannot be equated with an immaterial substance separated from our biological needs and physical desires. This is not to say that our essence can be properly understood solely on the basis of materialist criteria. Body and mind are interdependent entities. As the great German philosopher Immanuel Kant once put it, we humans stand with one foot in the world of things and with the other in the spiritual realm. Hence, both mind and matter must be taken into account in a proper analysis of the human condition. Indeed, as history has shown us over and over again, human action springs from both material and ideal interests. At the same time, however, let me reiterate that human nature cannot be dissociated from the biological dimension of our existence. To say that human nature is inherently flawed is, therefore, to acknowledge the fact that we necessarily engage in self-interested behavior in order to preserve our physical existence.

This leads me to address the second assertion contained in the first charge: the manifestation of human nature in the realm of politics and society. The biological imperative of self-preservation forces humans to engage in a ceaseless and violent struggle for existence. This is especially true in modern times. Our planet's population has increased and natural resources have decreased. As a result, the struggle for existence has intensified and become more violent.

Let me give you two concrete examples. For most of human history, wars were waged within certain geographical and technological limits. Hardly more than several thousand combatants faced each other in open battle. Today, millions of soldiers and civilians perish in global wars fought with insidious weapons of mass destruction. Only a few centuries ago, countless small economic entrepreneurs vied for the patronage of customers wealthy enough to buy their goods. Today, global corporations have eliminated thousands of small businesses as they compete with each other for market shares measured in billions of dollars.

Nowhere is this violent struggle for existence more visible than in the spheres of politics and economics. Hence, the first charge against nonviolence correctly points to the inevitability of violent action, *particularly in power politics*. Politics and power are connected insofar as politics is characterized by the striving for power or for influence on the distribution of power. In modernity, this quest for power occurs within a state as well as among states. The modern state, therefore, represents a large political association defined sociologically in terms of a means that is specific to the state, namely, physical violence. As citizens of the modern state we encounter the inevitability of violence every day in the form of the policeman on the street corner and the soldier in the garrison. Even a superficial consultation of basic history books reveals that every existing state today is founded on violence. The reason why we have states, and why we all live in states, lies, in the first place, in the fact that violence has been successfully normalized and institutionalized. At the moment violence is monopolized, civil wars end and states are born or reborn. Thus, all states are creatures of violence that exercise violence in return.

BOX 3.1

WEBER ON THE STRUGGLE FOR EXISTENCE

In the struggle for life, there is no peace to be had. The somber gravity of the population problem alone is enough to prevent us from imagining that peace and happiness lie waiting in the womb of future, and from believing that anything other than the hard struggle of man with man can create elbow room in this earthly life. As far as the dream of peace and happiness is concerned, the words written over the portal into the unknown future of history are: "Abandon all hope you who enter here."

The connection between human nature and violence should now be obvious. Because of their physical nature, humans are forced to participate in the violent struggle for existence. The modern state represents one important outcome of this struggle. Its political leaders—elected or self-appointed—wield power through the lawful exercise of violence. Usually, ordinary citizens obey the laws because they respect the authority of the state and fear its ability to unleash massive amounts of violence. The violent struggle for existence continues in the international arena as sovereign nation-states strive for global supremacy.

Let me now address the second charge: *Nonviolence does not work in the real world. The proof of the impracticality of nonviolence is that its proponents do not achieve their desired political and social goals.*

Who can deny the validity of this statement? I do not know of a single historical example of a proponent of nonviolence who achieved his desired political goals. In fact, most nonviolent leaders try to avoid power politics altogether. Jesus Christ is the most prominent example of such an apolitical proponent of nonviolence. In his famous Sermon on the Mount he formulates an *ethic of principled conviction* when he rejects the exercise of violence unconditionally. Indeed, the Gospels are pervaded by such an ethic that tells Christians to "resist not evil with force" and "turn the other cheek." These absolute moral injunctions are divine commandments that do not ask by what right the other person has struck you. The proponent of an ethic of principled conviction categorically rejects all action that employs violence.

In my view, this ethic makes sense only for saints and people who are more concerned with the eternal life in the beyond than with their temporary existence on earth. When Jesus admonished his followers to give Caesar his due he seemed to realize that nonviolent sainthood is incompatible with the achievement of political goals. He must have known that it was impossible to end the Roman occupation of ancient Judea by simply turning the other cheek. For this reason, he openly admitted that his kingdom was not of this world. Such a world-denying posture is the only response consistent with nonviolent principles. After all, in the imperfect world of power politics the decisive means is the use of violence. Unwilling to dilute his moral principles, Jesus eschewed the political arena and dedicated his short life to saving souls. Likewise, later Christian leaders who refused to abandon their political objectives eventually were forced to abandon their nonviolent principles.

The violence written into the very fabric of this world thwarts all efforts to establish a nonviolent society. Given that politics operates on the basis of power backed up by the use of violence, the person entering public life cannot help but become involved with the diabolical powers that lurk in all violence. Inevitably, the politician must follow a difficult path reflected in an *ethic of responsibility*. This ethic is governed by the maxim that you must resist what you consider evil with force, for if you don't, you are responsible for the spread of evil. Bound to this unavoidable contract with violent means to achieve concrete political ends, political leaders must accept the bloody consequences of their actions. Violence has to be done, and it is up to the individual to decide on how to do it. This fundamental insight is also reflected in the third charge: *Nonviolence does not provide adequate security. The refusal to employ defensive violence makes people far more vulnerable to their violent*

BOX 3.2
WEBER ON THE STATE
A state is that human community which successfully lays claim to the monopoly of legitimate physical violence within a certain territory. The state is held to be the sole source of the right to use violence.

BOX 3.3
WEBER ON VIOLENCE: MODERN REALISM
Anyone seeking to save his soul or the soul of others should not take the path of politics in order to reach this objective. The quite different task of politics can only be solved by violence. The genius—or demon—of politics lives in inner tension with the god of love.

neighbors and enemies. To opt for nonviolence means to neglect one's social responsibility and risk the safety of one's community.

Committed to an ethic of responsibility, the political person realizes what terrible political disasters can befall communities if they allow themselves to be seduced by the moral purism of the proponents of nonviolence. To be political means to make a conscious decision to remain in this world and participate in the never-ending struggle for existence. The refusal to do so results in the demise of the community at the hands of less-principled people. In other words, the most irresponsible of all means is the nonuse of any means.

As a warning, please consider the example of radical pacifist sects like the Quakers in Pennsylvania. Stubbornly adhering to their nonviolent principles, the Quakers refused to take up arms even at the outbreak of the American War of Independence in 1776. Fortunately, their revolutionary fellow citizens rose to the occasion and defended the very ideals the Society of Friends supposedly stood for: liberty, equality, solidarity, and peace. Had it not been for the valiant efforts of their violence-accepting compatriots, the Quakers might have lost the very religious freedoms that, in the first place, made possible their establishment as a distinct community of faith.

It is easy to sit on the high horse of nonviolence preaching peace and condemning those who exercise violence out of an admirable sense of responsibility for the survival of their national community. In fact, the refusal to endorse even defensive forms of violence contains a strong streak of hypocrisy. After all, pacifists enjoy the benefits that flow from their association with the modern state without acknowledging its inevitably violent foundation. Even worse, those who refuse to support their fatherland in the hour of need are unpatriotic moralists who undermine the necessary war effort and thus indirectly aid the cause of the enemy. It would be better for such people to simply get out of the way. Let them practice nonviolence in a monastery!

Believe me, I am not saying that all political activists are heartless creatures without ethical principles. In this respect, the ethic of principled conviction and the ethic of responsibility are not absolute opposites. But any political leader with a refined sense of responsibility for his community will accept the fact that there exists a tension between nonviolent principles and political power. Since these two impulses can never be fully reconciled, the political person is forced to resort to violence to protect the interests of his community—albeit reluctantly and with a heavy heart.

It is my hope that I have been able to convince you that political activity necessarily implies violence. The optimistic expectations of the Enlightenment philosophers notwithstanding, social and scientific progress has not resulted in the reduction of violence. In modernity, the struggle for existence has assumed more violent forms than in any other period of human history. Most honored jurors, please consider carefully the arguments offered in my testimony. I am sure that such a critical reflection will lead you to draw appropriate inferences. It is my expert opinion that nonviolence should be found guilty on all three charges.

Questions for Cross-examination

1. Weber admits that both mind and matter must be taken into account in a proper analysis of human nature. If that is so, why does his discussion of human nature focus exclusively on its physical dimension?

BOX 3.4
WEBER ON POLITICAL RESPONSIBILITY

It is immensely moving when a mature person who feels with his whole soul the responsibility he bears for the real consequences of his actions, and who acts on the basis of an ethic of responsibility, says at some point, "Here I stand, I can do no other."

---

2. Where does human cooperation fit into Weber's "struggle for existence"?

3. What kind of evidence does Weber offer for his claim that humans are forced to participate in a violent struggle for existence? Could not one's refusal to exercise violence be seen as an equally valid expression of human nature?

4. Even if Weber is correct in his assumption that the struggle for existence is unavoidable, does this necessarily mean that all forms of struggle must be violent?

5. Is Weber's early-twentieth-century assessment of the "population problem" a sound basis from which to predict with certainty that future peace and happiness are unattainable goals for humanity?

6. Weber claims that violence lies at the foundation of the modern state. Do we know with certainty that the modern state represents the ultimate framework of human community?

7. Weber links power to violence. Is this necessarily the case? Can there be nonviolent power?

8. Weber claims that he does not know of a proponent of nonviolence who achieved his desired political goals. Does this necessarily mean that such a person does not exist?

9. Even if Weber is right on the nonexistence of politically successful proponents of nonviolence, can one infer beyond reasonable doubt that such persons cannot emerge in the future?

10. How does Weber know that violence is the only effective way to defend a community from external aggression? Does the employment of violence guarantee a successful defense?

Suggestions for Further Reading and Thinking

Topic 1. Max Weber's Ideal Politician

In spite of his hard-nosed realism, Weber did not hesitate to speculate about what makes an ideal political leader. In his essay "The Profession and Vocation of Politics" he mentions passion, judgment, and sense of responsibility as the three decisive characteristics of such a person. For Weber, passion signifies both an intellectual concern and an emotional commitment to a political cause. Judgment refers to a person's psychological ability to maintain inner composure and calm while being receptive to the political requirements of the "real world." Political leaders exercise good judgment when they manage to maintain enough distance to things and other people. Finally, Weber argues that a strong sense of responsibility for the well-being of one's community represents the guiding pole star of appropriate political action.

The central difficulty of political leadership, according to Weber, is actually to put leaders into office who possess this rare combination of hot passion and cool judgment. Moreover, such leaders must have a sense of responsibility to keep them from succumbing to vanity—the mortal enemy of all dedication to the common good. Weber was convinced that the democratic process was the best vehicle for finding persons who possessed all three qualities.

Do you agree with Weber's arguments? Do you think he identified the right leadership qualities? Can you think of additional traits? A perusal of Weber's *Political Writings* will provide you with the necessary primary sources to answer these questions. In political science, the subject of leadership has been receiving growing attention. Indeed, as you will find out in later chapters of this book, the success or failure of certain political strategies often depends on capable leadership. As jurors in this important trial, therefore, it would behoove you to extend your understanding of political leadership. James McGregor Burns's classic study *Leadership* is an excellent place to start.

Suggested Reading

James MacGregor Burns. *Leadership*. New York: HarperCollins, 1985.

Wolfgang J. Mommsen. *The Age of Bureaucracy: Perspectives on the Political Sociology of Max Weber*. New York: Harper & Row, 1974.

Frank Parkin. *Max Weber*. New York: Routledge, 2002.

Max Weber. *Political Writings*. Ed. Peter Lassman and Ronald Speers. Cambridge, U.K.: Cambridge University Press, 1994.

Useful Web Sites

www.faculty.rsu.edu/~felwell/Theorists/Weber/Whome.htm

www.marxists.org/reference/subject/philosophy/works/ge/weber.htm

Topic 2. Max Weber and Social Darwinism

Like most of his contemporaries, Max Weber was deeply influenced by Charles Darwin's theory of evolution by natural selection. By the late nineteenth century, a number of social scientists applied some elements of biological evolutionism to explain the development of modern society. Herbert Spencer (1820–1903) was by far the most influential of these "Social Darwinists." Late in his life, he reported total sales of his books at close to 400,000 copies. For Spencer, capitalism constituted the most civilized form of human competition, in which the "fittest" would naturally rise to the top. By emphasizing the importance of the "struggle for existence" in his own writings, Weber, too, accepted a central tenet of Social Darwinism.

The late nineteenth century was also an era of globalization. Economic and cultural interactions among people in various geographical regions of the world accelerated and intensified. By rejecting state regulation of the economy, Social Darwinists, including Spencer, provided free-market capitalism with an important theoretical justification. After all, the depiction of free-market competition as the natural source of human freedom and prosperity served the interests of the commercial classes in Europe and the United States. In today's era of "turbocapitalism," following the collapse of the Soviet empire in 1991, Social Darwinist ideas have been making a strong comeback. This widespread celebration of ruthless competition, selfish individualism, and extreme consumerism is reflected in popular culture. As pointed out in the previous chapter, ubiquitous TV shows like *Survivor*, *The Weakest Link*, and *Dog Eat Dog* attest to the popularity of Social Darwinism in our own age of globalization.

Suggested Reading

Peter Dickens. *Social Darwinism: Linking Evolutionary Thought to Social Theory*. Cambridge, U.K.: Open University Press, 2000.

Richard Hofstadter. *Social Darwinism in American Thought*. Boston: Beacon Press, 1992.

Herbert Spencer. *Political Writings*. Ed. John Offer. Cambridge, U.K.: Cambridge University Press, 1994.

Recommended Visual Materials

Living in a Global World: Eight Questions About Globalization. Prod. James White, Honolulu, Hawai'i: Globalization Research Center, University of Hawai'i–Manoa, 2002. Video.

CHAPTER FOUR

REINHOLD NIEBUHR
Christian Realism

Historical Background and Credentials
of the Witness

Niebuhr's Testimony

Questions for Cross-examination

Suggestions for Further Reading and
Thinking

**Figure 4.1 Reinhold Niebuhr,
1892–1971. Courtesy of
Corbis.**

Historical Background and Credentials of the Witness

Reinhold Niebuhr was born in Wright City, Missouri, as the oldest son of German immigrants, Gustav and Lydia Niebuhr. Shortly after Gustav Niebuhr arrived in the United States in 1878, he attended Eden Theological Seminary in Missouri, an institution of higher learning associated with the German Evangelical Synod of North America. Gustav's piety and intellectual curiosity had a tremendous impact on his son's life. From the time he was a small child, Reinhold felt a strong attraction to the religious life. In 1912, he resolved to follow his father's example and enrolled in Eden Theological Seminary. He continued his studies at Yale Divinity School, where he received a master's degree. In 1915, the mission board of his denomination sent him to Detroit, where he served as pastor in a small congregation located in a poor working-class neighborhood.

Troubled by the miserable living conditions of his parishioners, most of whom were autoworkers in the nearby Ford plant, Niebuhr did not hesitate to speak out publicly against Henry Ford's exploitative employment practices. The young pastor also permitted union organizers to use his church as a hub of reformist political activity. After World War I, Niebuhr's liberal sentiments turned into outright pacifism. His antimilitaristic stance was reinforced during his 1923 visit to Europe, where he witnessed the devastating effect of the Great War on the physical and psychological health of ordinary German and French citizens.

In 1928, Niebuhr accepted the position of professor of practical theology at Union Theological Seminary in New York, leaving behind a thriving congregation in Detroit. Indeed, in his thirteen years as pastor, church membership had grown from 65 to 700. During the dark years of the Great Depression, Niebuhr became a leading advocate for a socialist interpretation of Christian teachings. He admonished his students to embrace the communitarian values of their faith and serve society by exposing the injustice of the capitalist system. In 1932, he published *Moral Man and Immoral Society*, a book that raised a storm of controversy and placed him in the public spotlight as one of America's most innovative theological thinkers.

Over the years, both his socialist and pacifist sympathies cooled off significantly. During World War II he even reversed his position on the subject of war and nonviolence by strongly supporting the Allies's war effort. Convinced that the evils of Nazism threatened the very existence of Western civilization, he argued that Hitler's acts of aggression could only be contained through a greater counterforce. Eventually, his views congealed around a position he called "Christian realism," or "biblical realism"—a perspective on the human condition that drew heavily on St. Augustine's teachings. Niebuhr articulated the central tenets of Christian realism most clearly in his later books, especially *The Nature and Destiny of Man* (1943) and *Man's Nature in His Communities* (1965). By the time he retired from Union Theological Seminary in 1960, his writings had deeply influenced American Protestant thought. A few days shy of his seventy-ninth birthday, Reinhold Niebuhr succumbed to heart failure in Stockbridge, Massachusetts.

Like the two previous expert witnesses for the prosecution, Niebuhr possesses impeccable credentials. In addition to publishing countless articles, he authored more than a dozen books on topics ranging from

Christian ethics and world history to international politics. Yet Niebuhr's main achievement—his articulation of modern Christian realism—was not merely an abstract position assembled in the ivory tower of academia. Rather, it grew out of his long years of experience as a pastor, social activist, union organizer, international lecturer, and trusted adviser to prominent politicians.

Most important, Niebuhr understands the appeal of nonviolence better than both Machiavelli and Weber. His early sympathies for pacifism and nonviolence exposed him to the most important literature on the subject available at the time. Thus, Niebuhr's testimony against nonviolence comes from intimate experience. Please listen carefully to the testimony of Professor Reinhold Niebuhr, our final expert witness for the prosecution.

Niebuhr's Testimony

Dear jurors,

I am grateful to be given the opportunity to address you in this important trial of nonviolence. You might wonder why a man of the church should appear before you as an expert witness for the prosecution rather than testifying on behalf of the defense. After all, the teachings of Jesus Christ are often seen as the prime examples for an uncompromising stance in favor of love, forgiveness, and nonviolence. No doubt, as a former pastor and professor of theology I cannot help but feel some sympathy for the cause of nonviolence and pacifism. Still, I fear that my understanding of our earthly existence and the conditions of spiritual liberation leave me with no other choice than to support the three charges against nonviolence. Indeed, it is precisely my intimate relationship to Christianity that leads me to criticize nonviolence from the perspective of Christian realism—a perspective perfectly compatible with the spirit of my religion. Let me start by commenting on the first charge: *Nonviolence is contrary to human nature. Since human nature is inherently flawed and sinful, people engage in violence. Moreover, our instinct for self-preservation compels us to compete for scarce resources, thus making violence inevitable in human affairs, particularly in power politics.*

I am afraid that the doctrine of nonviolence is based on an overly optimistic understanding of human nature. This naïve assessment is deeply rooted in the eighteenth-century views of Enlightenment philosophers such as Voltaire and Kant, who believed that human beings are essentially rational creatures. In addition, they assumed that people are infinitely malleable. Create the right social environment, they argued, and you will get decent human beings. Unfortunately, this one-sided conception of human nature has become the foundation of political and social attitudes that are dominant in modern liberal democracies. In their rationalistic pride, these liberal philosophers discarded the Christian doctrine of original sin. The latter, of course, points to the unavoidable presence of self-interested impulses and a will to power in all human beings, regardless of their cultural backgrounds. Every page of world history attests to the timeless wisdom contained in this doctrine.

At the same time, however, it would be a mistake to reduce human nature to base animal instincts. Although there always lurks a natural survival impulse at the core of all human ambitions, the instinct for self-preservation cannot be neatly separated from our need to socialize with our fellows and to become part of a community. In short, humans have capacities for both good and evil. To assume that individuals always assert their self-interest without regard to the whole is just as wrong as to suppose that persons can bring their egotistic tendencies under the permanent control of a higher law of love and nonviolence.

Overall, then, the biblical doctrine of original sin serves as the foundation for a Christian realism that rejects both the amoral cynicism of war realists like Machiavelli and the utopianism of liberal idealists who

---

BOX 4.1
NIEBUHR ON ORIGINAL SIN

Original sin is not an inherited corruption, but it is an inevitable fact of human existence. It is there in every moment of existence. No matter how wide the perspective the human mind may reach, how broad the loyalties which the human imagination may conceive, how universal the community which human statecraft may organize, or how pure the aspirations of the saintliest idealist may be, there is no level of human moral or social achievement in which there is not some corruption of inordinate self-love. This sober and true view of the human situation has been neatly rejected by modern culture.

BOX 4.2

NIEBUHR ON LOVE AND SIN: CHRISTIAN REALISM

Christianity is a religion which measures the total dimension of human existence not only in terms of the final norms of human conduct, which is expressed in the law of love, but also in terms of the fact of sin. It believes, in other words, that though Christ is the true norm for every man, every man is also in some sense a crucifier of Christ. In that sense, Christ is the "impossible possibility." Loyalty to him means realization in intention, but does not actually mean the full realization of the measure of Christ.

---

want to establish everlasting harmony on earth. As a corrective to these two extreme positions, Christian realism acknowledges the moral capacities of humans without forgetting the power of self-interest. It applauds our quest for peace while always reckoning with the forces of violence. Most important, Christian realists understand that the egoistic corruption of even our highest ideals is a much more persistent fact in human conduct than any proponent of nonviolence would be inclined to admit.

Although the first charge against nonviolence fails to mention the moral capacities of humans, it nonetheless correctly captures the inevitability of violence based on our inescapable sinfulness. As St. Augustine points out, the tension between Christ's law of love and human sinfulness cannot be resolved on earth but only in the beyond by the grace of God. Any Christian theology that fails to acknowledge the tragic factor of sin is sacrilegious, both from the standpoint of the Gospels and in terms of its blindness to the violent facts of human experience. We must do what we can to follow the law of love while recognizing that we are stricken by incurable pride and self-interest. Even a superficial study of the Gospels reveals that Jesus was perfectly aware of the fact that humans are frail and therefore can never completely overcome their sinfulness. That is why he forgave his closest disciple, Peter, who denied him three times. That is why he even absolved the cruel Roman soldiers who nailed him to the cross.

Yet, Jesus' acknowledgment of human sinfulness does not invalidate the truth of his absolute ethical imperatives to "love your enemies" or to "resist no evil." These injunctions remain the supreme and timeless moral law that ought to guide our conduct. At the same time, however, this human world of imperfection will always resist the full implementation of these commandments. For that reason, the New Testament interprets human history as a stage for the tension between love and sin to the end of time. Consequently, the realization of the Kingdom of God should be seen as a divine, not a historical, possibility. The persistence of the conflict between love and sin is the main reason why the proponents of nonviolence do not achieve their desired political and social goals. This recognition of the impracticality of nonviolence is, of course, the main point made in charge number 2: *Nonviolence does not work in the real world. The proof of the impracticality of nonviolence is that its proponents do not achieve their desired political and social goals.*

Even a moral and honest person like Mahatma Gandhi could not prevent the massive outbursts of violence that followed the 1947 partition of the Indian subcontinent into India and Pakistan. Ultimately, Gandhi's nonviolent approach fell short of its objectives because politics, by definition, deals with the self-interest of individuals or groups. Any attempt to work out these conflicting interests will at best lead to fleeting compromises that will eventually give way to new power struggles. Political activity can never be expected to lead to some sort of final harmony. Let us not forget that power has to do with whatever decisions people make about the arrangements under which they live. As St. Augustine wisely reminds us, the pursuit of power takes place in what he calls the "earthly city"—our temporary abode characterized by tension, friction, and clash of interests. Its mode of operation is pride, domination, greed, and violence.

In fact, the idea that proponents of nonviolence are capable of pursuing political objectives amounts to a contradiction in terms. Why? Because every political objective, every political situation, demands involvement in self-interest, power, and, therefore, violence. An ethic of pure nonviolence can have no immediate relevance to any political situation. This is also the central insight expressed in the final charge: *Nonviolence does not provide adequate security. The refusal to employ defensive violence makes people far more vulnerable to their violent neighbors and enemies. To opt for nonviolence means to neglect one's social responsibility and risk the safety of one's community.*

Since human egoism makes a world of perfect nonviolence impossible, to maintain social order governments must coerce deviant individuals.

Logical consistency demands from proponents of nonviolence that they advocate the abolition of the entire judicial process in society because of its violent and coercive character. But does it make sense for any civilized community to dispense with the mechanisms of corrective violence? Of course not. Unless we are willing to condone the suffering of innocent people, we must continue to put criminals in jail. On this point, the supposed immorality of using violence against any human being cannot outweigh the social benefits that accrue from cracking down on crime. Admittedly, there remains always the risk of legitimate violence turning into tyrannical force. On the other hand, we must not underestimate the danger of any society's disintegrating into utter anarchy and chaos. It is precisely in the midst of such insoluble dilemmas that we truly appreciate the insights of Christian realism, for it allows us to accept that human existence is characterized by the impossibility of living risk-free.

As far as the employment of defensive violence against external aggressors is concerned, I wholeheartedly agree with the view expressed in charge number 3: the failure to do so amounts to neglecting one's social responsibility. This does not mean that we have to call such large-scale forms of defensive violence "just wars." On this point, I do not fully agree with St. Augustine. Wars may never be completely just, but some wars are necessary.

Consider, for example, the context of German aggression that provoked World War II. We now know that the policy of appeasement

---

BOX 4.3
ST. AUGUSTINE'S JUST-WAR DOCTRINE
According to St. Augustine, wars are just if they meet the following conditions:

1. There must be competent authority to order the war for a public purpose.
2. There must be a just cause such as self-defense or the protection of rights.
3. The means must be proportionate to the just cause.
4. All peaceful alternatives must have been exhausted.
5. There must be right intention on the part of the just belligerent.

practiced by Great Britain, France, and other European powers in the 1930s only emboldened Hitler to order the invasion of more countries. Can anyone seriously argue that nonviolence would have stopped his armies of evil? To the contrary, the refusal to employ defensive violence would have led to the unification of Europe under the Nazi swastika. Fortunately, the Allies did not listen to the proponents of nonviolence. Instead, they recognized their moral responsibility to frustrate the Nazi effort to achieve world dominance. The destructive power of Nazi Germany had to be checked by greater Allied counterforce. I admit that the defeat of Nazi Germany and the empire of Japan was a bloody task. Moreover, it did not guarantee the emergence of a new world order free of tyrants, dictators, or terrorists. But the battle against the evils of fascism was a destructive enterprise that could not be avoided—unless, of course, we are prepared to abdicate our communal responsibility in the name of nonviolent purity.

Dear jurors, I would like to close this testimony by asking you to remember that human history is inextricably involved in sin and violence. We find no release from guilt and violence except in the grace of God. This does not mean that we are given license to sin as we please. Quite to the contrary, our devotion to God binds us to the highest moral principles—even if we continuously fail to embody them fully. The lover of peace in the tradition of Christian realism knows that knowledge of God's moral law is no guarantee of people's ability or willingness to obey it. We are all involved in a rebellion against God—a rebellion too

---

BOX 4.4
NIEBUHR ON THE BALANCE OF POWER
The balance of power is a basic condition of justice, given the sinfulness of men. Whenever an individual or a group or a nation possesses undue power, and whenever this power is not checked by the possibility of criticizing and resisting it, it grows inordinate. Such a balance of power does not exclude love. In fact, without love the frictions and tensions of a balance of power would become intolerable. But without the balance of power even the most loving relations may degenerate into unjust relations, and love may become the screen that hides injustice.

---

serious to be overcome by the rosy optimism of nonviolence. Hence, it is my expert opinion that nonviolence should be found guilty on all three charges.

Questions for Cross-examination

1. What evidence does Niebuhr offer for the validity of his doctrine of original sin?
2. Can "realism" be based on religious faith? Is Niebuhr's Christian realism a contradiction in terms?
3. Niebuhr admits that the first charge against nonviolence fails to mention the moral capacities of humans. If this is so, doesn't this omission prove that the first charge is at least partially flawed?
4. Why must "tension, friction, and clash of interests" in the "earthly city" necessarily lead to violence? Aren't there many historical examples that show the viability of forms of conflict resolution that do not involve violence?
5. Niebuhr claims that any pursuit of political objectives involves self-interest, power, and, therefore, violence. Is his use of the word "therefore" justified? Do self-interest and power necessarily, and in all cases, entail violence?
6. Niebuhr argues that it does not make sense for any civilized community to dispense with the mechanisms of corrective violence. Is violence the only possible means of social correction? How does Niebuhr know that corrective violence is a better means of preventing the suffering of innocent people than nonviolent mechanisms?
7. Does one's refusal to employ defensive violence necessarily imply one's refusal to defend one's community by other means?
8. Niebuhr implies that nonviolence is tantamount to passivity and appeasement. Is that a fair assessment of nonviolence? What about nonviolent forms of resistance such as labor strikes, economic boycotts, and civil disobedience?
9. Niebuhr argues that without the balance of power even the closest relations may degenerate into unjust relations. Could it also be argued that the balance of power can contribute to an escalating arms race among nations?

Suggestions for Further Reading and Thinking

Topic 1. Should Christians Embrace Pacifism?

In 1940, Reinhold Niebuhr published an essay that bore the provocative title "Why the Christian Church Is Not Pacifist." The thesis of the article is that the failure of the Christian church to espouse pacifism is not a deplorable deviation from the true faith. Rather, it is anchored in a realistic understanding of the Christian Gospel expressed not merely in the law of love but also in the fact of sin. Hence, Christians ought to avoid the utopian illusion of achieving perfect love in a sinful world and instead embrace Christian realism. Niebuhr concluded that Christians who celebrate unconditional pacifism and the ideal of nonviolence as the core of Jesus' teachings mistakenly turn their religion into the heresy of earthly perfectionism.

But there are quite a number of Christians who disagree with Niebuhr's interpretation. In fact, entire Christian denominations such as the Mennonites and the Society of Friends (Quakers) have been built on the principles of unconditional pacifism and nonviolence. Some theologians have pointed out that early Christians up until the fourth century regarded love and nonviolence as the essence of Jesus Christ's teaching. For example, during that early period, most Christians refused service in the Roman army. Moreover, there is no direct evidence that they ever used force against the bloody persecutions to which they were subjected. By and large, early Christians were willing to share the martyrdom of Jesus. Remarkably, their suffering seemed to have had an extraordinary effect in converting many of those who witnessed their martyrdom. It was only when the Roman emperors Constantine and Theodosius made Christianity into the official religion of the empire that its newly empowered clergy found religious justifications for acts of cruelty, war, and violence that were committed in the name of Christ.

Should Christians embrace pacifist values? What do you think? The literature below has been selected to help you answer this question. You might want to start with a perusal of the selected essays and addresses compiled by Robert McAfee Brown in *The Essential Reinhold Niebuhr.* As in the case of Machiavelli and Weber, two accessible biographies, by Robert W. Lovin and Richard Wrightman Fox, give you a more in-depth portrait of the witness. K. S. Latourette's dated but invaluable *A History of the Expansion of Christianity* tells a fascinating story of the early

Christians' pacifism. Finally, David Smoch's *Perspectives on Pacifism* provides an important comparative perspective.

Suggested Reading

Richard Wrightman Fox. *Reinhold Niebuhr: A Biography*. Ithaca, N.Y.: Cornell University Press, 1997.

K. S. Latourette. *A History of the Expansion of Christianity*. Vol. 1, *The First Five Centuries*. New York: Harper & Bros., 1937.

Robert W. Lovin. *Reinhold Niebuhr and Christian Realism*. Cambridge, U.K.: Cambridge University Press, 1995.

Reinhold Niebuhr. *The Essential Reinhold Niebuhr: Selected Essays and Addresses*. Ed. Robert McAfee Brown. New Haven: Yale University Press, 1986.

David R. Smoch, ed. *Perspectives on Pacifism: Christian, Jewish, and Muslim Views on Nonviolence and International Conflict*. Washington, D.C.: United States Institute of Peace, 1997.

Recommended Visual Materials

The Shakers: Hands to Work, Hearts to God. Dir. Ken Burns and Amy Stechler-Burns. Florentine Films and WNET (New York), 1985.

The Good War and Those Who Refused to Fight It. Prod. and dir. Rick Tejada-Flores and Judith Erlich. Transit Media, 2002.

Bonhoeffer: Agent of Grace. Dir. Eric Till. NFP Teleart, 2000. Video.

Useful Web Sites

www.leaderu.com/isot/docs/niehbr3.html
www.witnessforpeace.org
www.nisbco.org
www.pbs.org/faithandreason/theogloss/radref-body.html

PART II

The Expert Witnesses for the Defense

CHAPTER FIVE

MAHATMA GANDHI
Militant Idealism

Figure 5.1 Mahatma Gandhi, 1869–1948, M.K. Courtesy of Gandhi Institute for Nonviolence, Memphis, TN.

Historical Background and Credentials of the Witness

Gandhi's Testimony

Questions for Cross-examination

Suggestions for Further Reading and Thinking

Historical Background and Credentials of the Witness

The youngest of five children, Mohandas Karamchand Gandhi was born into a merchant-caste family residing in the Indian port town of Porbandar. His father was the chief administrator of this tiny princely city-state and was married to a deeply religious woman belonging to a sect that combined Hindu and Muslim beliefs. Mohandas's mother also welcomed Jains and Christians in her house, so the boy grew up in an open climate of religious toleration. After his father's untimely death during his high school years, the young man resolved to study law in London. To receive the blessings of his mother, Mohandas had to promise her he would avoid wine, meat, and sex during his stay in England. After three difficult years of study, Gandhi was called to the bar in 1891.

He immediately returned to his home country to practice his profession. After a brief and unsuccessful legal career in Bombay and other Indian cities, Gandhi accepted a one-year position as litigation lawyer for a thriving trading firm in South Africa, owned by Muslim merchants of Indian extraction.

Subjected to an intense climate of racial discrimination, Gandhi decided to fight back, thus finding his calling as a civil rights activist. Eventually he brought his wife, Kastur, and his children to South Africa and accepted an offer made by a group of wealthy Indian businesspeople in Durban to direct a comprehensive legal campaign aimed at repealing racist laws against Indian immigrants. Guided by liberal ideals of equality and social justice, he founded important political organizations such as the Natal Indian Congress, several centers of communal living, one being his ashram near Durban, and *Indian Opinion*, a weekly serving the Indian community in South Africa.

At the same time, however, Gandhi demonstrated his unwavering loyalty to the British Empire and its professed liberal philosophical principles. He volunteered as a medic in the British army during the Boer War (1899–1902) and served in the same position during the 1906 British expedition against the Zulu resistance movement. Unfortunately, both his exemplary war service and his numerous legal petitions on behalf of South African Indians failed to transform the racist attitude of many government officials. Pushed to experiment with more radical measures of direct political action, Gandhi arrived in 1907 at his famous method of *satyagraha* ("truth-force")—a militant form of active nonviolent resistance employing peaceful demonstrations, strikes, boycotts, and acts of civil disobedience. Refusing to submit to racist laws that subjected Indians to humiliating registration requirements, Gandhi and his followers willingly accepted personal suffering in the form of substantial fines, jail sentences, and physical abuse.

In spite of these unjust punishments, Gandhi's method caught on. Thousands of ordinary South African Indians participated in various *satyagraha* campaigns, eventually forcing the South African regime to repeal some of its most discriminatory measures. In 1909, at the height of his struggle for racial justice, Gandhi wrote *Hind Swaraj (Indian Independence)*, a political and spiritual treatise that severely criticized the materialist tendencies of modern civilization. His faith in the Empire weakened and he began to explore his own cultural heritage. Having

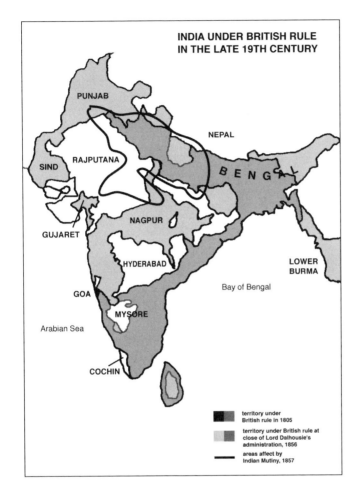

INDIA UNDER BRITISH RULE
IN THE LATE 19TH CENTURY

PUNJAB

NEPAL

SIND RAJPUTANA

B E N G A L

NAGPUR

GUJARET

HYDERABAD

LOWER
BURMA

GOA

Bay of Bengal

MYSORE

Arabian Sea

COCHIN

territory under
British rule in 1805

territory under British rule at
close of Lord Dalhousie's
administration, 1856

areas affect by
Indian Mutiny, 1857

Figure 5.2
Colonial India
in the Late
Nineteenth
Century.
Courtesy of
Author.

greatly simplified both his lifestyle and his dress, Gandhi returned to India in 1915. No longer the awkward Bombay lawyer in a Western suit who was too shy to conduct tough cross-examinations of witnesses, Gandhi had been turned by his political struggle in South Africa into a prominent public figure in Indian life poised to unleash the method of *satyagraha* in the ongoing national struggle for independence.

Within a few years, Gandhi managed to unify the many factions of the unruly Indian National Congress under his firm leadership. Known as the "Mahatma" ("great soul"), he preached Hindu-Muslim friendship and championed the integration of the outcastes, or "untouchables," into

Indian society. In preparation for political independence, he challenged Indians of all social and religious backgrounds to undergo a process of moral purification and social regeneration. From 1920 to 1922, Gandhi spearheaded a resistance movement calling for nonviolent noncooperation with the British colonizers. Millions of ordinary Indians joined the struggle and the only reason the movement failed to achieve its ultimate political objective was that a small number of demonstrators violated their nonviolence pledge. Unwilling to bring about Indian independence through violent methods, Gandhi called off the entire campaign and was promptly arrested by the British, who sentenced him to an extended prison term on the charge of sedition.

As soon as he was released, however, Gandhi reentered politics. Over the next two decades he organized two large civil disobedience movements: the famous 1930–31 "Salt Satyagraha" and the 1942–44 "Quit India" campaign. Even when the British finally granted India its independence after World War II in 1947, the Mahatma saw little reason to celebrate this milestone in modern Indian history. Unable to settle their differences, the Muslim and Hindu leadership had agreed to partition the subcontinent along religious lines into the Muslim-dominated Pakistan and the Hindu-led India. Refusing to accept the finality of this decision, Gandhi dedicated what were to be the last few months of his life to ending the communal violence that had erupted all over India in the wake of partition. Still weakened by a long fast he had undertaken to underscore the urgency of communal peace, Gandhi was assassinated en route to a public appearance by a Hindu fundamentalist who believed that the Mahatma's plan for Hindu-Muslim unity was destroying India's Hindu identity.

The founder of the modern tradition of militant nonviolent direct action that bears his name, Gandhi represents the star witness for the idealist defense. His expertise in legal affairs, medicine, philosophy, politics, and social activism allows him to bring a variety of perspectives to the trial of nonviolence. Moreover, his status as a colonial subject adds an important personal understanding of violence and oppression to his testimony. Finally, his lifelong efforts as a mediator between opposing political, cultural, and religious camps speak to his grasp of the pragmatic dimension of politics. Please give your full attention to Mahatma Gandhi's arguments.

Gandhi's Testimony

Dear jurors,

I convey to you my warmest greetings. Please allow me to express my great appreciation for your willingness to hear me out. You have been asked to ascertain beyond all reasonable doubt whether nonviolence is guilty as charged. This is not an easy task. For one, the political stakes are very high. Think of it. If you find nonviolence guilty, then you basically acknowledge that love and goodwill represent but abstract notions that are inapplicable to the "real world" of politics. As a result, you would legitimize the violent social status quo on our planet. If, on the other hand, you find nonviolence not guilty, then you admit that humans can do much better than habitually resorting to the path of violence and destruction. Such an admission would expose the inadequacy of the violent political systems and social structures that exist in the world today. Naturally, your exoneration of nonviolence would lend moral support to those of us who call for fundamental change in the ways by which humans conduct their political affairs. In either case, your verdict has great political and moral significance. This is why your task is not easy.

As someone who has dedicated his entire life to the nonviolent transformation of unjust social structures, I fervently hope that my testimony will convince you to find nonviolence not guilty as charged. To be sure, to many people such a verdict would appear to be contrary to common sense. As you well know, however, appeals to common sense have often served to legitimate oppressive social practices. Aristotle's arguments in favor of "natural slavery" reflected common sense in ancient Greek society. Likewise, the Church-sanctioned belief in the divine right of kings corresponded to medieval common sense.

Enough said by way of introduction. Let me present my views with regard to the first charge: *Nonviolence is contrary to human nature. Since human nature is inherently flawed and sinful, people engage in violence. Moreover, our instinct for self-preservation compels us to compete for scarce resources, thus making violence inevitable in human affairs, particularly in power politics.*

This charge expresses the common view that humans are deeply flawed and driven to violence by their animalistic instincts for physical self-preservation. As evolutionary biologists have pointed out, humans and animals do share common origins. Surely, the strength of our animalistic drives is a constant reminder of the awesome power of biology. Nonetheless, the realist spirit behind the first charge grossly simplifies and distorts reality by reducing human nature to animalistic violence. Why does it refuse to acknowledge the slow process of social and moral evolution that has led many people to cultivate self-restraint for the benefit of others? The alleged impossibility of ridding ourselves of sin stands in stark contrast to the experience of real people who have managed to better themselves under effort and discipline. There is no good reason for limiting humanity's capacity for moral improvement. Moral improvement may be a slow process, but to cite a mere lack of speed is not an adequate argument against the possibility of a nonviolent politics.

For this reason, I maintain that humans are not bound to instinct and brute force like unreflective animals. There is no question that human nature contains violent impulses, but it also holds the opposite qualities of gentleness and love. Think of emergency situations when people often sacrifice their lives to rescue complete strangers. How else can we explain such actions except by assuming that, in addition to our selfish tendencies, we also possess a profound sense of our interconnectedness? Moreover, do not the sacrifices our parents have made on our behalf point to the existence of instincts quite different from the ones described in the first charge?

Dear jurors, please keep in mind that my arguments in favor of love and goodwill are not predicated on the denial of instincts geared to preserve our physical existence. Obviously, we need to kill living organisms to live. Thus, a certain amount of violence is built into the human con-

---

BOX 5.1
GANDHI ON MORAL IMPROVEMENT
Man has by painful striving to surmount and survive the animal in him, and from the tragedy of the violence which is being acted around him, he has to learn the supreme lesson of nonviolence for himself. Man must, therefore, if he has to realize his dignity and his own mission, cease to take part in the destruction and refuse to prey on his weaker fellow creatures.

dition. But does this mean that we can deduce from our need for physical sustenance the inevitability of violence, "particularly in power politics"? Of course not. Why? Because the deterministic language of charge number 1 completely ignores the element of human choice. We may have to kill in order to live, but we can choose to limit such necessary forms of violence to edible plant species. I cannot detect any "natural" imperative that requires us to take human or animal life to ensure our physical survival. Likewise in the realm of politics we can choose to pursue power by either violent or nonviolent means. There is no natural or divine law that dictates to us that we must kill each other. Quite to the contrary, all major world religions emphasize commandments that expressly forbid us to kill.

It seems to me that individuals always possess the power of choice. The particular circumstances and historical conditions in which we find ourselves might make one choice easier than another, but the possibility of choice always remains. Added together, these countless moments of choice lead either to the increasing brutalization of our character and our environment or to our growing awareness of the dignity and worth of every single human being. Reliance on violence—be it instinctual or psychological violence—is always a sign that we have opted to disregard the bonds that connect us and instead feed the flames of egotism that cut us off from other people. Alternatively, by affirming the truth of interconnectedness, we acknowledge the spiritual oneness of all humanity. The air we breathe, the water we drink, the food we eat—even these basic activities are constant reminders of our involvement in the interdependent and divine whole that many people call God or Truth.

Let me now turn to the second charge: *Nonviolence does not work in the real world. The proof of the impracticality of nonviolence is that its proponents do not achieve their desired political and social goals.* Apparently we are to understand the phrase "does not work" as indicating the ineffectiveness or impracticality of nonviolence as a political means. In short, it is asserted that nonviolence does not get us what we want in politics. By implication, one has to assume that, for the realist prosecution, violence represents an effective or at least a *more effective* political means. But does violence really work as well as is often unquestioningly assumed by realists? In fact, historical evidence does not support such assumptions. Sometimes violence seems to "work" in the sense of helping certain groups to achieve their political objectives, but often it fails miserably. Ironically, in some cases the increased exercise of violence translated into diminishing political returns. For example, violence did not work in the case of the British Empire's seeking to secure its colonial rule over India. The growing willingness of colonial government to rely on the power of their guns only strengthened the resolve of Indians to resist. Violence also proved to be a highly ineffective tool in the hands of the Catholic church during the Inquisition. Instead of silencing dissenters and so-called heretics, it only added fuel to the flames of the Reformation. And the list of violence's failures goes on and on.

"But Mr. Gandhi," some of you jurors might interject, "why do you bring up the ineffectiveness of violence? Nonviolence is on trial, not violence!" Fair enough. Let me explain. The reason why I discussed the ineffectiveness of violence is because this question reveals a serious flaw contained in the second charge. If we want to evaluate the effectiveness of nonviolence as demanded by the prosecution, then we need to think much harder about what precisely constitutes a success or failure of any political method, violent or nonviolent. It is simply not true that nonviolence represents an ineffective or impractical means in the political arena. Like violence, it may "work" better or worse in different circumstances. However, when given a fair chance to be implemented, the nonviolent militancy of *satyagraha* has proven to be highly effective in helping groups in society to achieve their political goals. Let me give you an example.

In 1907, the government of Transvaal in South Africa passed the notorious Black Act, which introduced limitations on the free movement of Indians, required Indians to submit to humiliating registration procedures, and imposed an annual tax on formerly indentured Indian laborers. A few years later, the South African Supreme Court added insult to injury by declaring Hindu, Muslim, and Parsee marriages invalid, thus branding all Indian wives mistresses and their children bastards. Naturally, the Indian community in South Africa was outraged. We vowed to engage in militant nonviolent direct action to pressure the government to repeal these measures. Hundreds of Indian *satyagrahis* crossed the state border separating the states of Transvaal and Natal, thus deliberately breaking the unjust law restricting their freedom of movement. Others went to jail for burning their registration cards or refusing to submit to the humiliating registration requirements. Thousands of Indian miners went on strike in solidarity with the impris-

oned resisters. In 1914, the South African government finally withdrew
the requirement for Indians to register and carry passes. In addition, the
tax on laborers was abolished, the system of indenture was to cease per-
manently, and all marriages were recognized. On the issue of movement
and immigration restrictions we achieved a compromise: the restrictions
were eased, but not abolished altogether.

In short, the nonviolent method of *satyagraha* turned out to be an
extremely effective and practical means for social change. The Indian
practitioners of militant nonviolence in South Africa achieved their
desired political goals. This impressive example taken from the "real
world," dear jurors, should make you pause and reject the faulty
assumptions contained in the second charge. Please remember the
instructions you received at the beginning of this trial. As a former
lawyer, I know them very well. If there exists direct or circumstantial evidence that casts doubt on the veracity of a particular charge, you must
find the defendant not guilty with regard to this charge. I believe I have
just presented you with such evidence.

Finally, let me address myself to the third charge: *Nonviolence does
not provide adequate security. The refusal to employ defensive violence
makes people far more vulnerable to their violent neighbors and enemies. To opt for nonviolence means to neglect one's social responsibility
and risk the safety of one's community.*

In some cases, it may be true that defensive violence protects the
noncombatant members of the community from the harmful actions of
the invader. The imperatives of modern warfare, however, dictate that
combat necessarily infringes upon the civilian sphere. Moreover, as I

BOX 5.2
**GANDHI ON THE EFFECTIVENESS OF NONVIOLENCE
EVEN WHEN USED BY SIMPLE COUNTRY FOLK**
I remember an instance when, in a small principality, the villagers
were offended by some command issued by the prince. The former
immediately began vacating the village. The prince became nervous,
apologized to his subjects and withdrew his command. Many such
instances can be found in India.

BOX 5.3

GANDHI ON NONVIOLENCE AND BRAVERY

To fight with the sword does call for bravery of a sort. But to die is far braver than to kill. He alone is truly brave, he alone is a martyr in the true sense who dies without fear in his heart and without wishing to hurt his enemy, not the one who kills and dies. Heroic as it undoubtedly is for a handful of people to offer armed resistance in the face of superior numbers, it is far more heroic to stand up against overwhelming numbers without any arms at all.

---

have stated before, a sustained military defense effort may actually increase the aggressor's willingness to raise the level of violence. We have witnessed such escalations of violence during World War II when Nazi Germany stepped up its bombing raids on London to break the resolve of the defenders or when the United States dropped two nuclear bombs on Hiroshima and Nagasaki to force the empire of Japan to surrender unconditionally.

I don't mean to suggest that people simply ought to remain passive and let the invader have its way. This would be not nonviolence but cowardice. *Satyagraha*, militant nonviolence, is active resistance based on the virtue of courage. Like the violent method, it demands sacrifice and suffering on the part of the resisters, but unlike the violent method, its practitioners refuse to kill or injure, thus breaking the endless cycle of violence and counterviolence.

The refusal to obey the aggressor's orders combined with the bravery of exerting active, nonviolent pressure has repeatedly proved its ability to enhance the safety of the community by forcing the invading power to withdraw its forces. Let me give you an example.

At the beginning of World War II, German military forces descended on Denmark, easily overpowering the weak Danish defense forces. The Danish government's swift surrender led the Nazi occupiers to decide to keep it in place as long as its members followed their orders. Soon, an underground movement formed with the clear objective of offering nonviolent resistance to the Germans, in the form of consumer boycotts, work slowdowns, and open acts of noncooperation. As Danish defiance intensified, Hitler gave the Danish government a tough ultimatum: proclaim a state of emergency and put an end to all forms of resistance or the country will be placed under direct German military rule. The government refused to go along and all members of the cabinet resigned. Over the next months, German troops meted out harsh punishments to resisters. To their great surprise, however, Danish defiance increased. Although there were occasional acts of violent sabotage, most actions organized by the Danish resistance remained nonviolent. Executions and other violent reprisals only hardened the opposition. Unable to coerce the Danes into obedience, German occupation forces never gained full control over the country.

The Danish example proves two points relevant to the third charge. First, no matter how terrible the aggressor faced by those relying on the method of *satyagraha*, military measures are not powerful enough to put down a popular movement. Resilient and imaginative nonviolent direct action eventually takes a significant financial and psychological toll on the invader. Thus, contrary to charge number 3, the refusal to employ defensive violence does not make people easy targets for their violent neighbors and enemies. Second, the Danish example shows that nonviolent resistance can strengthen a community's sense of solidarity and determination. To opt for nonviolence, therefore, is not necessarily tantamount to neglecting one's social responsibility and risking the safety of one's community.

Dear jurors, please reflect carefully on the arguments and examples you have heard in my testimony. It is my expert opinion that nonviolence should be found not guilty on all three charges.

BOX 5.4
GANDHI ON *SATYAGRAHA* AND POLITICAL RULE
In politics, the use of *satyagraha* is based upon the immutable maxim that government of the people is possible only so long as they consent either consciously or unconsciously to be governed.

Questions for Cross-examination

1. Even if Gandhi is correct in assuming that human nature contains both good and evil tendencies, does not the very existence of some negativity in our essence suggest that we will always be prone to engage in violence?
2. What evidence does Gandhi offer for humanity's alleged capacity for moral improvement?
3. Aren't there certain situations—for example, being suddenly attacked—that do not allow for the necessary moment of reflection that precedes making a conscious choice between violence and non-violence?
4. What evidence does Gandhi provide for the alleged "truth of inter-connectedness" and the "spiritual oneness of all humanity"?
5. Gandhi's *satyagraha* campaign in South Africa may have resulted in partial success and some compromises, but the ultimate political objective—the complete repeal of all discriminatory laws against Indians—was not achieved by the time Gandhi returned to India. How can partial success and compromise be considered achieving one's political objectives?
6. With regard to the Danish example, isn't it likely that the nonvio-lent resisters could have been more easily controlled if Nazi Germany had not had to fight a violent war against the Allies? Thus, wasn't the valiant nonviolent effort of the Danes bolstered by exter-nal violence?
7. Isn't it possible that the Danish defiance increased because the Germans were losing the war and not because of the effectiveness of their method?
8. Does Gandhi rely too much on rare cases? Aren't there many examples that show that military measures can be powerful enough to put down a popular movement, violent or nonviolent?
9. What if the aggressor is willing to kill the entire population of a country? How can the method of nonviolence ever provide adequate protection against such a ruthless enemy?

Suggestions for Further Reading and Thinking
Topic 1. Gandhi and the Bhagavad-Gita

All of Gandhi's earthly possessions consisted of two pairs of sandals, his loincloth, a blanket, a pocket watch, eating utensils, a pair of wire-rimmed glasses, three little ivory monkeys, and three holy books: the Bible, the Koran, and the *Bhagavad-Gita*. Usually translated as "Song of the Lord," the *Gita* was undoubtedly Gandhi's favorite book. He often referred to it as Mother because it nourished his spirit and taught him the *yoga*, or "yoke," of action. A central portion of the ancient Indian epic *Mahabharata*, the *Gita* presents a dialogue between the princely warrior, Arjuna, and the god Krishna, who has assumed human form as the prince's charioteer. Arjuna is reluctant to lead his army into battle because the enemy is made up of his own kinsmen and led by his own cousins. Noticing his hesitancy, Krishna advises the prince to fulfill his *dharma* (duty) as a warrior in a selfless, detached way. He should neither take pleasure in killing nor should he reject *karma* (action). Recognizing the charioteer's divinity, Arjuna realizes that by performing his warrior *dharma* with absolute devotion to Krishna, he can unite with God's cosmic purpose and free himself from the blinding egotism that binds humans to the endless cycle of birth and death. By achieving a mental state of complete selflessness, Arjuna would be able to put an end to further rebirths and thus reach *moksha* (liberation).

Traditional Hindu interpretations emphasize *dharma* and the inevitability of doing one's duty according to one's caste, even if it includes the taking of human life. Gandhi fundamentally disagreed. For the Mahatma, the story of Arjuna and his divine charioteer did not describe a real event. Rather, it was an allegory pointing to the psychological battle between good and evil that rages inside all of us. Reaching beyond the narrow framework of caste duties, the *Gita* taught the way of *karma yoga*—selflessness in spirit and action. Gandhi believed that this ideal of desirelessness demanded from every single person a commitment to develop inner peace, moral righteousness, and compassion. In this way, then, the *Gita* serves as the inspiration for a life committed to nonviolence. Needless to say, many orthodox Hindu priests categorically rejected Gandhi's interpretation.

What do you think? Read Barbara Stoler Miller's translation of the *Gita* and judge for yourself. It won't take you more than two hours to read through this short, inspirational story (it is available in many different editions and translations). The *Gita* will also help you understand why Gandhi engaged in stringent mental and physical forms of discipline that included sexual abstention, extensive walks, and frequent fasts. Make sure to peruse the excellent studies by J. T. F. Jordens and Margaret Chatterjee, respectively, of Gandhi's approach to religion. Also make sure to familiarize yourself with Gandhi's works as edited by Raghavan Iyer. The shortest and most accessible introduction to Gandhi's life and thought is Bhikhu Parekh's excellent *Gandhi*. Don't forget to watch the 1982 movie *Gandhi*. Ben Kingsley's brilliant portrayal of the Mahatma earned him an Academy Award for Best Actor.

Suggested Reading

Joan V. Bondurant. *Conquest of Violence: The Gandhian Philosophy of Conflict*. Princeton, N.J.: Princeton University Press, 1988.

Judith Brown. *Gandhi: Prisoner of Hope*. New Haven: Yale University Press, 1989.

Yogesh Chadha. *Gandhi: A Life*. New York: John Wiley, 1997.

Margaret Chatterjee. *Gandhi's Religious Thought*. Notre Dame, Ind.: University of Notre Dame Press, 1983.

M. K. Gandhi. *Hind Swaraj and Other Writings*. Ed. Anthony J. Parel. Cambridge, U.K.: Cambridge University Press, 1997.

Mahatma Gandhi. *The Essential Writings of Mahatma Gandhi*. Ed. Raghavan Iyer. Delhi: Oxford University Press, 1993.

J. T. F. Jordens. *Gandhi's Religion: A Homespun Shawl*. New York: Palgrave, 1998.

Barbara Stoler Miller, trans. *The Bhagavad-Gita: Krishna's Counsel in a Time of War*. New York: Bantam Books, 1986.

Bhikhu Parekh. *Gandhi*. Oxford, U.K.: Oxford University Press, 1997.

Ronald Terchek. *Gandhi: Struggling for Autonomy*. Lanham, Md: Rowman & Littlefield, 1998.

Useful Web Sites

www.gandhiinstitute.org

www.mkgandhi.org

web.mahatma.org.in/flash.html

Topic 2. Gandhi's Nonviolent Nationalism

Struggling against British colonialism in India, Gandhi dedicated his life to the creation of a benign nationalism that would propel India into independence without violence. As the history of the Indian nationalist movement shows, however, the nationalist fervor of the masses often conflicted with the Mahatma's nonviolent message. Is it consistent to support the particularistic agenda of one's nation and yet remain wedded to a universalistic ethic of nonviolence? Are patriotism and nonviolence mutually exclusive commitments? What do you think?

The books listed below offer different interpretations of Gandhi's own struggle to reconcile nonviolent principles and nationalist power. The important topic of nationalism and its relationship to (non)violence relates directly to a number of arguments that have been made by our expert witnesses.

Suggested Reading

Partha Chatterjee. *Nationalist Thought and the Colonial World*. Minneapolis: University of Minnesota Press, 1995.

Dennis Dalton. *Mahatma Gandhi: Nonviolent Power in Action*. New York: Columbia University Press, 1993.

Anthony J. Parel, ed. *Gandhi, Freedom, and Self-Rule*. Lanham, Md: Lexington Books, 2000.

Manfred B. Steger. *Gandhi's Dilemma: Nonviolent Principles and Nationalist Power*. New York: Palgrave, 2000.

Topic 3. Gandhi's Ascetic Practices

From the time he decided to devote himself to the nonviolent struggle against racism in South Africa, Gandhi began to experiment with a number of ascetic practices, including fasting, extreme vegetarianism, sexual abstention, and other strict physical regimens. Several times in his life he used extreme fasting as one of his nonviolent methods to achieve political objectives. Some commentators have suggested that such fasts are actually violent because they contain a clear element of coercion. Gandhi, however, denied that his fasts were coercive because they were not undertaken for a selfish purpose. Moreover, he maintained that fasting involved self-suffering without causing or intending any physical or material harm to the opponent.

Does fasting coerce people into actions that they would not otherwise have endorsed? What do you think? Find below a number of books that offer helpful perspectives on this difficult question.

Suggested Reading

Joseph S. Alter. *Gandhi's Body: Sex, Diet, and the Politics of Nationalism.* Philadelphia: University of Pennsylvania Press, 2000.

Erik H. Erikson. *Gandhi's Truth: On the Origins of Militant Nonviolence.* New York: W. W. Norton, 1969.

Susanne Hoeber Rudolph and Lloyd I. Rudolph. *Gandhi: The Traditional Roots of Charisma.* Chicago: University of Chicago Press, 1983.

Ved Mehta. *Mahatma Gandhi and His Apostles.* New York: Viking, 1977.

Recommended Visual Materials

Gandhi. Dir. Sir Richard Attenborough. 1983. Feature film.

"Gandhi: Pilgrim of Peace." Episode on A&E *Biography* series. Available on video.

"India: Defying the Crown." Episode on PBS series *A Force More Powerful: A Century of Nonviolent Conflict.* Available on video.

CHAPTER SIX

MARTIN LUTHER KING, JR.
Christian Idealism

Figure 6.1 Martin Luther King, Jr.,
1929–68. Courtesy of Corbis.

Historical Background and Credentials of the Witness

Martin Luther King, Jr. was born into a religious black middle-class family in Atlanta, Georgia, as the oldest son of Alberta King and Martin Luther King. The pastor of Ebenezer Baptist Church in Atlanta, King's father was a charismatic orator and engaged community leader. He was also active in the National Association for the Advancement of Colored People (NAACP) at a period when this civil rights organization had begun to challenge deeply engrained Jim Crow laws and practices in the South. Most white Americans in this region regarded the NAACP as a dangerously "radical association" bent on "causing trouble" and "disrupting" the southern way of life.

Martin was an extraordinarily gifted and articulate child who from the age of five was irresistibly drawn to the ministry as he proudly watched his father delivering fiery speeches from the church pulpit.

Licensed by his father to preach at the tender age of 18 and ordained to the Christian ministry only a few months later, King graduated from Atlanta's Morehouse College in 1948 with a bachelor's degree in sociology. After receiving a second bachelor's degree in divinity from Crozer Theological Seminary in Chester, Pennsylvania, he was accepted as a graduate student at Boston University's School of Theology. In 1955, after five years of intense study, King received his doctorate in systematic theology at the age of 26.

Throughout his student years, King was profoundly influenced by a number of thinkers. For example, Benjamin Mays, president of Morehouse College, impressed on the young minister the urgent mission of modernizing the black church through a combination of educational efforts and political activism. L. Harold De Wolf, King's mentor at Boston University, admonished him to view God as an intimate force operating in persons who take individual responsibility for bettering the world by resisting moral and social evil. King was also drawn to the turn-of-the-century writings of Walter Rauschenbusch, a famous theology professor at Rochester Theological Seminary who had been the leading voice of the anticapitalist "social gospel movement," which was dedicated to bringing about a true Christian commonwealth based on morality, equality, solidarity, and simplicity. The writings of the German philosopher Georg W. F. Hegel taught King that social conflict and tension were not problems, to be avoided at all cost, but that they often served as indispensable catalysts for progressive historical change. Searching for an appropriate means of changing society in accordance with Christian principles of love and nonviolence, King encountered Gandhi's method of *satyagraha* through lectures given by Mordecai Johnson, president of Howard University, and A. J. Muste, a professor at Crozer. As King would later put it, "Jesus furnished the spirit and motivation and Gandhi furnished the method." Eager to learn more about Gandhi's techniques of nonviolence, King and his wife, Coretta, later spent a month in India as invited guests of Prime Minister Nehru.

In 1954, King became the pastor of the prestigious Dexter Avenue Baptist Church in Montgomery, Alabama. A year later he was thrust onto the world-historical stage when he resolved to lead the struggle against appalling practices of racism and segregation in his adopted hometown. Rosa Parks, a black seamstress and active member of the local NAACP chapter, had refused to surrender her seat in a city bus to a white rider, thus breaking a segregationist city ordinance and implicitly challenging the underlying Jim Crow system in the South. Coming on the heels of the U.S. Supreme Court's 1954 ruling against public school segregation in *Brown vs. Topeka, Kansas Board of Education*, Park's courageous act provided the spark for what would soon turn into a nationwide African-American struggle for civil rights. For 381 days, King led a successful nonviolent boycott by blacks of the Montgomery public transit system that ultimately led to the desegregation of the system.

Two years later, King institutionalized the newly acquired social power of his movement by founding the Southern Christian Leadership Conference (SCLC), a civil rights organization based in hundreds of black churches throughout the South. In 1960, King resigned from his Montgomery parish to become copastor in his father's church in Atlanta. This allowed the young civil rights leader to dedicate himself completely to the struggle at hand. Spearheading boycotts, strikes, and demonstrations against racial segregation throughout the South, King consciously courted arrest to expose racial injustice and arouse the conscience of white America. His famous "Letter from Birmingham City Jail" represents one of the most eloquent statements ever written in defense of taking nonviolent direct action against the evils of racism and segregation. On August 28, 1963, King delivered his famous "I Have a Dream" speech before a huge national television audience and a quarter of a million participants in the March on Washington, an event organized to pressure Congress to enact massive civil rights legislation. A year later, King received the Noble Prize for Peace and witnessed President Lyndon B. Johnson's signing of the Civil Rights Act of 1964—a crucial step toward dismantling Jim Crow.

In the last four years of his life, King's leadership in the Civil Rights Movement was increasingly challenged by Malcolm X, Stokely Carmichael, and other militant black voices who advocated the pursuit of "Black Power" by any means necessary. Although King recognized the resilience of racism in the United States, he never abandoned his commitment to the nonviolent method. As the Vietnam War heated up in the mid-1960s, King became an outspoken critic of the United States's imperialist foreign policy. Exposing the social and economic roots of racism and injustice, King announced in 1967 the formation of an SCLC-led "Poor People's Campaign" with the aim of easing the plight of the poor, regardless of the color of their skin. His last nonviolent direct action involved leading six thousand protesters on a march through downtown Memphis in support of striking sanitation workers. On April 4, 1968, Martin Luther King, Jr., was assassinated by James Earl Ray, a white racist.

Considered by many as the most significant spiritual and political successor of Gandhi, King is one of the most eloquent expert witnesses to appear in this trial. As will become apparent in his testimony below, his idealist interpretation of politics contrasts with Niebuhr's realist perspective. Less of an academic theologian than Niebuhr, King nonetheless wrestled with difficult philosophical and religious problems. His life cut short by the bullet of his assassin, King's practical experience as a committed nonviolent leader spans a period of thirteen years. Like the witnesses before him, the American civil rights leader interacted with many prominent political and religious figures of his time. Thinking that he could serve his nonviolent cause best by remaining as close to ordinary people as possible, he never accepted political office. Let us listen to Dr. Martin Luther King, Jr., the second expert witness called by the defense.

King's Testimony

Dear jurors,

I understand that this has been a long trial. Given that some of you must be tired and exhausted by now, I am overwhelmed by your obvious willingness to give me your undivided attention. I very much appreciate it. I promise to do my best to make my testimony as succinct and focused as possible. Let me turn without delay to the first charge against nonviolence: *Nonviolence is contrary to human nature. Since human nature is inherently flawed and sinful, people engage in violence. Moreover, our instinct for self-preservation compels us to compete for scarce resources, thus making violence inevitable in human affairs, particularly in power politics.*

As a young graduate student at Boston University, I encountered the Christian realism of Reinhold Niebuhr. His writings left a deep impression on me. Thanks to the arguments made by this great American theologian, I realized that my idealistic optimism concerning human nature had frequently caused me to overlook the fact that reason is often darkened by sin. Although my childhood experiences in the segregated South had taught me about the power of human selfishness and cruelty, I held a rather superficial optimism concerning human nature. Niebuhr's theology was a necessary reminder of the reality of sin on every level of human existence. After reading his books, I found it difficult to quarrel with his argument that our biology makes us finite children of nature. In other words, the physical aspects of our existence subject us to the laws of nature—a realm of necessity where coarse bodily desires and fear of physical pain often interfere with our higher spiritual inclinations. Thus humans are in perpetual need of repentance for their failings, particularly for the sin of intellectual and spiritual pride.

But the recognition of our biological and moral limitations does not mean that we should accept the one-sided generalization of human nature offered in the first charge. We are more than just our biology. There is an amazing potential for goodness in human nature. I find it both dangerous and erroneous for modern Christians to cling to an exaggerated pessimism that is mired in questionable concepts of biological determinism and spiritual inadequacy. Why should we resign ourselves to the idea that humans are helpless creatures who, through their misuse of freedom, have irretrievably lost their goodness? If we are really created by God, how can the image of the divine in us be totally effaced to the point where we are incapable of escaping violence and ruthless competition? Have we forgotten that Jesus Christ constantly appealed to a hidden goodness in even the worst criminal? Obviously, the Son of God would not have made these efforts had he been convinced that we are inherently flawed and sinful. If anything, Jesus showed us that God is a personal force that works both in the hearts of people and in the real world of politics. Behind the harsh appearances of the world there is a benign power.

BOX 6.1
KING ON THE IDEA OF A PERSONAL GOD

To say that God is personal is not to make him an object among other objects or to attribute to him the finiteness and limitations of human personality; it is to take what is finest and noblest in our consciousness and affirm its perfect existence in Him. So in the truest sense of the word, God is a living God.

BOX 6.2
KING ON FREE WILL

We must believe that man has the power of choosing his supreme end. He can choose the low road or the high road. He can be true or false to his nature.

My disagreement with Niebuhr and the Christian realists begins precisely with the question of where love stands with respect to human nature. Rather than letting ourselves be overwhelmed by grim interpretations of original sin based on orthodox notions of predestination, we modern Christians ought to embrace the uplifting message of the New Testament. Since each one of us has been created in the image of a loving God, we all have the capacity to turn away from evil and realize our potential for goodness. To do that, however, we must consciously act on the basis of love and reason. To be rational means to be free to choose. And with rational choice comes ethical responsibility. To affirm love, reason, choice, and responsibility is, therefore, to reject the realist claim of the inevitability of violence and the absolute dominance of animal instincts.

Contrary to the harsh vision of human nature expressed in the first charge, Christianity affirms the existence of love at the core of our being. This uplifting affirmation is what I consider to be the central message of a sensible Christian idealism—one that is wisely tempered by a sense of humility in the face of our shortcomings. To say that love is our innermost, divine essence means not only to acknowledge love as the highest moral good but also to affirm it as the highest reality pervading the universe. As John the Evangelist says, "God is love." So how can any genuine Christian agree with the claim that nonviolence is contrary to human nature? Moreover, the life of Jesus shows that there exists a direct link between love and nonviolence. Responding to acts of violence in kind constitutes a flagrant violation of Jesus' moral injunction to love our enemies. But let me be crystal clear here. In this context, I am not referring to love as some sentimental emotion. It would be nonsense to urge people to love those who inflict violence on them in an affectionate sense. "Love" in this connection means something akin to "goodwill."

There are three words for "love" in the Greek New Testament. In Platonic philosophy, *eros* refers to the yearning of the soul for the realm of the divine. In modern times, *eros* has come to mean a sort of aesthetic or romantic love. *Philia* denotes a love that is based on reciprocity such as the intimate affection that exists between friends. Finally, *agape* refers to a form of love that expresses itself in wishing people well. Biblical theologians might say it is the love of God working in the minds of humans. I am quite certain that it is this more general kind of love Jesus had in mind when he admonished us to love our enemies.

At this point some of you might want to raise an obvious objection to my remarks thus far. What about non-Christians? What about atheists? How can a theory of human nature based on Christian love have any relevance for such people? Well, it seems to me that love and justice are relevant to all human beings. In fact, anybody who holds that justice is better than injustice anchors this judgment in some ideal that cannot be proved empirically. In this sense, then, even the atheist who is committed to justice shows faith. We may call the object of faith truth, higher law, idea, brahman, god, or dharma. It does not matter what term we use, because all of them connote a form of universal connectedness based on *agape*, or goodwill. By the way, realists, too, profess to prefer justice to injustice. Thus, we can safely conclude that they must also be committed to *some* deep ideal of human community that runs counter to the grim picture of human nature evoked in the first charge.

Let me bring up one final point in regard to this charge. By equating power with violence, realists simply assumed that the ultimate expression of power is violence. Thus, they argue, power politics is inconceivable without violence. This reflects a very poor understanding of power. Power, properly understood, is the ability to achieve purpose. It is the strength required to bring about social, political, and economic changes. As the civil rights movement has shown, this strength does not

---

BOX 6.3
KING ON *AGAPE*

Agape means nothing sentimental or basically affectionate; it means understanding, redeeming good will for all men, an overflowing love which seeks nothing in return. When we love on the agape level, we love men not because we like them, not because their attitudes and ways appeal to us, but because God loves them.

BOX 6.4
KING ON LOVE AND POWER
One of the greatest problems of history is that the concepts of love and power are usually contrasted as polar opposites. Love is identified with resignation of power, and power with a denial of love. What is needed is a realization that power without love is reckless and abusive and that love without power is sentimental and anemic. Power at its best is love implementing the demands of justice.

---

necessarily grow out of the barrel of a gun. Goodwill combined with the willingness to suffer can be at least as strong a force as violence.

The nature of the relationship between power and nonviolence is also a theme raised in the second charge: *Nonviolence does not work in the real world. The proof of the impracticality of nonviolence is that its proponents do not achieve their desired political and social goals.* Throughout my life I have been a committed proponent of nonviolent resistance to evil. Have I achieved my desired political and social goals? Certainly not all of them. But who ever does? No doubt, in 1968, a large portion of white America was still poisoned by racism. The nation as a whole still needed to do much more to address the burning questions of race relations, poverty, militarism, and materialism. But does this mean that I have been unsuccessful in all my nonviolent endeavors? You be the judge of that. From my perspective, it seems obvious that nonviolence has been both a moral and a practical weapon. It is moral because it thrives on love rather than hatred. It does not want to humiliate its opponents; it wants to win their understanding. It seeks to redeem rather than injure. As for the practicality of the nonviolent method, what better proof is there than the American civil rights movement? Employing a creative range of nonviolent strategies, the civil rights activists accomplished many significant political and social goals, including the legal desegregation of the South and the passage of national civil rights legislation.

Think, for example, of the successful nonviolent boycott of the Montgomery public bus system, which lasted more than a year and ended in triumph for the black community. Consider the marches, demonstrations, and lunch-counter sit-ins we held in Birmingham, Alabama, to protest the city's racist segregation ordinances. Even the police chief Bull

Connor's attack dogs and water cannons could not prevent thousands of nonviolent demonstrators from reaching their political objective—the desegregation of the city. Recall the bravery of scores of "freedom riders" who spearheaded the successful campaign to integrate the interstate bus system. Take into account the successful efforts of thousands of nonviolent demonstrators in Selma, Alabama, who marched for voting rights and refused to be turned around by violent police tactics.

It is true, brave civil rights workers in Mississippi were killed, schoolhouses and churches throughout the South were bombed, and innocent children were murdered for no other reason than the color of their skin. Hundreds of the committed soldiers of nonviolence were viciously beaten. Thousands were jailed. Millions withstood the seemingly endless stream of racial slurs and insults. But in the end, even the most vicious racists were unable to stop the advance of the forces of justice. Violence failed to overcome the organized power of nonviolence. Racial hatred and blind rage proved to be no match for the nonviolent power of love.

Anyone who is even vaguely familiar with the history of the civil rights movement should be able to draw the obvious conclusion: the assumptions contained in charge number 2 are incorrect and, therefore, misleading. Indeed, they have been proved wrong in the real world of politics, not only in colonial India but also in Jim Crow America.

This leaves only the third charge to be discussed: *Nonviolence does not provide adequate security. The refusal to employ defensive violence makes people far more vulnerable to their violent neighbors and enemies. To opt for nonviolence means to neglect one's social responsibility and risk the safety of one's community.*

BOX 6.5
KING ON THE EFFECTIVENESS OF NONVIOLENCE
Nonviolence is a powerful and just weapon. It is a weapon unique in history, which cuts without wounding and ennobles the one who wields it. It is a sword that heals. With a practical and moral answer to the oppressed people's cry for justice, nonviolent direct action proved that it could win victories without losing wars.

This charge is predicated on the tacit assumption that violence does provide adequate security. This is a dangerous illusion that has been proved wrong by concrete historical events innumerable times. Just consider the twentieth century. The violence of imperialism and colonialism gave birth to World War I. The inconceivable violence of this unprecedented conflict begat the even greater violence of World War II. Out of this conflagration of death and destruction arose the Korean War, the Cold War, and the Vietnam War. What conclusion can we draw from this global escalation of violence? For one, it seems to be fair to say that meeting violence with retaliatory violence does nothing but intensify the existence of evil in the world. Violence begets violence; cruelty begets greater cruelty. Violence is incapable of eradicating other acts of violence. Only love can break the chain reaction of violence.

Again, when I speak of love, I mean *agape* expressed in a nonviolent struggle against evil. If we band together in such a struggle, we create a community more tightly knit than any group engaged in defensive violence. After all, the first objective of *agape* is to preserve and create community. Given that charge number 3 explicitly refers to "community," it is essential, dear jurors, that you consider the deeper meaning of this concept. In my view, a community should not be confused with a collection of individuals who have banded together mainly for the purpose of protecting their personal and collective self-interest. Indeed, most wars have been waged to champion narrow group interests and thus maintain global structures on inequality benefiting the few.

Conversely, a true community worth the name does not end at arbitrarily drawn political borders. Ultimately, it encompasses all members of our species. This all-inclusive human community comprises many smaller communities that are pervaded by a vision of total interrelatedness expressed in people's awareness that what directly affects one member affects all others indirectly. Such a community could be called a "beloved community," because it draws on the spirit of *agape* to determine the quality of its social relationships. Its laws, actions, and attitudes do not reduce persons to mere means or instruments but treat them as ends in themselves endowed with the right of rational self-determination. Persons are judged by the content of their character, not by the color of their skin. The bonds among the members of such a beloved community are perpetually rejuvenated by the persistent willingness of its members to sacrifice their narrow self-interest for the common good. How can we ever create or protect such a community with violence? Have we forgotten that the means we employ always affect the end we seek?

Some of you may think that I am hopelessly naïve and idealistic. The perfect community based on love and solidarity will never come about, you may think. Even if it did, such an ideal would still serve the indispensable political and moral purpose of guiding human societies in the direction of greater justice and equality. Don't get me wrong; I firmly believe that people have not only the right but also the moral obligation to resist violent aggressors. But, for both moral and pragmatic reasons, they ought to do so nonviolently. The closer a community moves toward the ideal of the beloved community, the harder it will be for enemies to achieve their violent objectives. Rather than neglecting one's social responsibility, therefore, one's participation in nonviolent direct action against the aggressor strengthens the collective sense of solidarity. The civil rights movement has demonstrated this point over and over again.

I know it is difficult to contemplate alternatives to deeply engrained, long-standing patterns of behavior. But viable alternatives to violence do exist. It is your duty, members of the jury, to weigh the evidence presented to you in this trial and find nonviolence not guilty on all three charges.

Questions for Cross-examination

1. Even if humans do possess an "amazing potential for goodness," is it possible that this potential might remain largely unrealized? In that case, does violence become "inevitable in human affairs"?
2. Is King's perspective on human nature entirely anchored in theological rather than rational arguments?
3. Does the realists' preference for justice indeed require them to hold an ideal that runs counter to their "grim picture of human nature"? What about the argument that just social arrangements serve people's purely pragmatic concerns for safety and self-preservation better than unjust ones?
4. King warns against taking extreme positions on human nature and "letting ourselves be overwhelmed by grim interpretations of original sin." Is he following his own advice or is he letting himself be overwhelmed by naïve interpretations of *agape*?

5. As King himself points out, the most important social and political goal of his nonviolent campaigns was to end racism in America. Did he succeed? If not, what does this tell us about the effectiveness of the nonviolent method?

6. If nonviolence was, indeed, such an effective tool in the civil rights movement, why did several members of the SCLC-affiliated Student Nonviolent Coordinating Committee revert to a qualified endorsement of violence in their struggle for racial equality?

7. What evidence does King offer for his assertion that a nonviolent, "beloved" community will make it more difficult for aggressors to achieve their violent objectives?

8. If, as King admits, the "beloved community" is a mere ideal to be approximated in the real world, does this mean that *agape* and nonviolence, too, represent ideals that can never be fully realized? In that case, will some violence always remain in human affairs?

9. Does King fully explain how nonviolence can provide adequate security for human communities?

Suggestions for Further Reading and Thinking

Topic 1. King Versus Eight White Alabama Clergymen

In April 1963, King found himself in a cell in the Birmingham City Jail for violating antidemonstration injunctions. He had been in town since February to lead the local campaign to desegregate all areas of city life. On April 16, King's attorneys brought him a copy of the local newspaper, which carried two statements about the campaign. One was written in support of King and signed by more than sixty local black leaders. The other statement was signed by eight white Christian and Jewish clergy of Alabama, led by C. J. Carpenter, the Episcopal bishop of Alabama. Issuing "an appeal for law and order and common sense" in dealing with racial problems in Alabama, the clergymen argued that the protests were unwise and untimely and were led in part by "outsiders." Moreover, they accused King and the other local black leaders of engaging in actions that were not truly "nonviolent" but were designed to incite hatred and violence. They ended their appeal by "strongly urging" the Negro community to withdraw support from these demonstrations.

Reading this statement in his cell, King decided to respond to it immediately, jotting down notes in the margins of the newspaper. The result was King's famous "Letter from Birmingham City Jail," an eloquent defense of the civil rights movement that had profound historical and symbolic import. King rebutted the "outsider" argument by noting that an injustice anywhere was a threat to justice everywhere, hence outsider activity to oppose unjust laws not only was welcome in Alabama but was the moral duty of any decent citizen in the country. Laying out the four steps of any nonviolent campaign—collection of facts to determine injustices, negotiation, self-purification, and direct action—he emphasized that nonviolent direct action was not generating violence but actually bringing to the surface the racial hatred and violence that was deeply embedded in social structures. He also noted that nonviolent direct action was designed to establish a "creative tension" in order to open the door to negotiation. Finally, he responded to the argument that the Birmingham campaign was "unwise" and "untimely" by pointing out that actions to remedy injustices had never been "well-timed," according to the timetable of the oppressor. As he put it, "For years now I have heard the word 'Wait!' It rings in the ear of every Negro with piercing familiarity. This 'Wait' has almost always meant 'Never.'"

Familiarize yourself with the most important speeches and writings of Martin Luther King, Jr. In addition to consulting two useful collections edited by James Washington you may also want to read at least one of the biographies listed below, by Stephen Oates, James Colaiaco, or Michael Dyson. King's philosophy of nonviolence is explained in an accessible and yet comprehensive manner in books by Greg Moses and John Ansbro. For a visual experience of King and his times, check out Johnson and Adelman's awesome collection of photos, or watch the PBS series *Eyes on the Prize* or the short but informative A&E *Biography* video.

Suggested Reading

John J. Ansbro. *Martin Luther King, Jr.: The Making of a Mind.* Maryknoll, N.Y.: Orbis Books, 1982.

James A. Colaiaco. *Martin Luther King, Jr.: Apostle of Militant Nonviolence.* New York: St. Martin's Press, 1988.

Michael Eric Dyson. *I May Not Get There with You: The True Martin Luther King, Jr.* New York: Touchstone, 2000.

Charles Johnson and Bob Adelman. *King: The Photography of Martin Luther King, Jr.* New York: Viking, 2000.

Greg Moses. *Revolution of Conscience: Martin Luther King, Jr., and the Philosophy of Nonviolence.* New York: Guilford, 1997.

Stephen B. Oates. *Let the Trumpet Sound: The Life of Martin Luther King, Jr.* New York: Plume, 1982.

James M. Washington, ed. *A Testament of Hope: The Essential Writings and Speeches of Martin Luther King, Jr.* New York: HarperCollins, 1986.

James M. Washington, ed. *I Have a Dream: Writings and Speeches That Changed the World.* New York: HarperCollins, 1992.

Recommended Visual Materials

Eyes on the Prize: America's Civil Rights Years. PBS series, 1986. Available on videocassette.

"Martin Luther King, Jr." Episode in A&E *Biography* series. Available on videocassette.

Martin Luther King, Jr.: A Historical Perspective. Dir. Thomas Friedman. Xenon Entertainment Group, 1994. Videocassette.

The Speeches of Martin Luther King, Jr. Prod. Darrell Moore. MPI Home Video, 1990. Videocassette.

Useful Web Sites

www.thekingcenter.org
www.stanford.edu/group/King
www.life.com/Life/mlk/mlkpics.html
http://almaz.com/nobel/peace/1964a.html

CHAPTER SEVEN

THE MOTHERS OF THE PLAZA DE MAYO
Anarchist Idealism

Figure 7.1 The Mothers of the Plaza de Mayo. Courtesy of Corbis.

Historical Background and Credentials of the Witnesses

From the mid-1960s to the late 1980s, military governments in Latin America systematically and brutally violated human rights as defined by the international community in 1948 when it adopted the Universal Declaration of Human Rights. Tens of thousands of people were arrested without formal charges being brought against them and were held at secret locations, and denied legal advice and a fair trial. Many of them were raped, tortured, and murdered. One of the most vicious of these Latin American authoritarian regimes was the military dictatorship that ruled Argentina with an iron fist in the late 1970s. On March 24, 1976, three high-ranking generals staged a successful overthrow of the democratically elected government headed by President Isabel Peron. Within months, a military junta headed by an army general, Jorge

Rafael Videla, suspended Congress, appointed sympathetic judges, banned all political parties, canceled elections, censored the press, and dissolved hundreds of civic associations.

Calling themselves the "guardians of national values," the military dictators drew upon St. Augustine's just-war theory to justify waging, what came to be termed, a "Dirty War" against citizens who might oppose their rule. Labeling such persons as leftists, subversives, or terrorists, the generals formed special commando units with the objective of capturing and interrogating the members of suspect organizations, their sympathizers, and their alleged associates. The stage was set for one of the worst periods of state terror and human rights violations recorded in modern history. But to wage its Dirty War without compromising its image abroad, the junta had to hide its brutality and rely on its deadly policy of "disappearing" suspects. Dragged from their homes and working places, a total of about fifty thousand people were shoved into unmarked cars headed for unknown destinations. When family members and friends tried to find out about the fates of their loved ones, authorities turned them away without explanation and threatened them with "serious consequences" if they did not stop their inquiries. In other words, throughout this ongoing nightmare of terror and repression, Argentine citizens were pressured to put up a deceptive front of "normalcy" and conduct their daily affairs as if nothing was happening. Cowed into silence, even those most affected by political repression seemed to have lost their will to resist the military dictatorship.

This pervasive climate of fear, paranoia, passivity, and acquiescence was abruptly shattered on April 30, 1977, when fourteen middle-aged women appeared on the Plaza de Mayo, the central square in downtown Buenos Aires, fronted by the presidential palace, the cathedral, and tall corporate buildings. Circling the towering pyramid at the center of the square with arms locked, the women held up pictures of the disappeared and carried signs that read, "Where are our children?" and "We demand an answer!" Over the next years, these "Mothers of the Plaza de Mayo" returned to the main square every Thursday in defiance of police orders. Although the women were brutally persecuted by the regime, their numbers grew and their strategies of nonviolent resistance became ever more sophisticated. Who were these "Mothers" and what were their goals?

The life of Hebe de Bonafini, the president of the Mothers organization, serves as a representative example for most of these women's social background. Hebe grew up in Buenos Aires in the early 1930s on an unpaved street in front of a hat factory where her father worked until he became disabled with arthritis. Suffering the economic hardship of a family that struggled to make ends meet, the girl nonetheless enjoyed the rich social life of a tightly knit community. Despite her dreams of acquiring a college education, Hebe never went beyond primary school because her father could only afford to send one child—her brother—to high school. As a young woman Hebe married the owner of a small mechanic workshop in the neighborhood. Helping out her husband in the shop and raising three children took up most of Hebe's energy during the next two decades. Although she still longed for the education required to become a teacher, Hebe ultimately accepted the traditional patriarchal Latin American values that kept women focused on household, family, and the church. Her modest life was shattered in 1976, when her son Jorge, an aspiring college teacher studying for a degree in electronic engineering, was "disappeared" by the regime. His "crime" consisted of socializing with progressive Catholics who believed that Jesus' teachings of love, fairness, and equality were meant to benefit especially the poor.

Hebe despaired at her son's disappearance. She simply could not understand why ten men dressed in civilian clothes and traveling in unmarked cars had trashed Jorge's apartment, threatened his wife, and dragged her son away without an explanation. She and her family went from police station to police station, only to be told that there was no official information about the incident. Unwilling to accept the loss of her son, Hebe kept searching. But things got worse. Perhaps as a consequence of her persistence, her second son, Raul, and Jorge's wife were also disappeared. But rather than breaking her will to find out the truth, these tragedies transformed Hebe de Bonafini into a powerful public voice for justice. She joined the Mothers organization and helped establish tight connections among other mothers whose loved ones had been disappeared, ultimately turning a loose affiliation of grieving women into a politically active and effective organization. Emerging as one of the group's chief planners, Hebe tirelessly traveled around the country, always encouraging ordinary people like her to resist the regime by "speaking truth to power." Never preparing her speeches in advance, she simply told her fellow citizens about the creation of the Mothers organization, how the women resolved to go out into the streets to find their children, and what they could do to fight the oppressive junta by nonviolent means. Bombarded with anonymous death threats, Hebe only narrowly escaped the fate of the disappeared a number of times. Some of her fellow Mothers were not as lucky; Azucena de Vincente and others disappeared into secret jails, where they were tortured and killed by government agents.

Still, their organization grew in numbers and stature. Soon it was no longer possible for the junta to arrest and kill Mothers without attracting international attention. In 1983, after Argentina's defeat in the Falkland War against the United Kingdom, the military dictatorship finally collapsed. But when President Raul Alfonsin's new, democratically elected government showed suspicious reluctance to prosecute all of those responsible for the Dirty War, the Mothers vowed to continue their struggle until every single disappeared person was accounted for. By the turn of the century, the Mothers organization was still active. In fact, it had turned into a powerful humanitarian organization dealing with human rights violations all over Latin America.

Unlike our previous witnesses, the Mothers do not possess impressive academic or diplomatic credentials. Like Hebe, most of the women are middle-aged and come from lower-middle-class backgrounds. Until their involvement with the Mothers organization, they had never been politically active. And yet, through their incredible courage and their commitment to nonviolent social change, they belied the dominant view in traditional, patriarchal societies that women, children, and the aged are weak and powerless, and should stay out of the public realm altogether. Their spirited struggle against a totalitarian state not only earned them international admiration but also made them experts in the strategy and tactics of nonviolent direct action.

Unlike Gandhi's nonviolent movement in India or King's civil rights movement in the United States, the Argentine resistance movement inaugurated by the Mothers was not dependent on a single charismatic leader. Rather, it was structured in a decentralized fashion, thus allowing each member to exert leadership. This egalitarian spirit, the hallmark of their anarchist idealism, was the glue that held together their organizational network.

Let us now listen to our final expert witnesses for the defense, the courageous Mothers of the Plaza de Mayo.

Testimony of the Mothers

Dear jurors,

We are very honored to be called before you to present our views. This is an important trial and we hope that our testimony will help you to come to a fair verdict. Before we address the three charges against nonviolence in more detail, please let us remind you that we are a human rights organization independent of any political party or group. Our expertise rests neither on extensive philosophical training nor on high political office. We are here because we are experts on how to employ various nonviolent methods against a repressive and brutal political regime that systematically tortured and killed its own citizens for no other reason than to enhance its own political power. We did not assemble these practical forms of political knowledge from books or pamphlets, although some of us enjoy reading—particularly historical novels and anarchist political writings. Rather, our expertise is rooted in the real world of power politics and has been refined in a painful process of trial and error.

Let us begin by addressing the first charge against nonviolence: *Nonviolence is contrary to human nature. Since human nature is inherently flawed and sinful, people engage in violence. Moreover, our instinct for self-preservation compels us to compete for scarce resources, thus making violence inevitable in human affairs, particularly in power politics.*

We suppose that philosophers and priests could offer you long, eloquent treatises on human nature. We can't do that because we don't know much about theology or metaphysics. To be sure, we're Catholics and Jews who believe in the existence of a just and merciful God. Most of us also accept and cherish Jesus Christ's message of love and redemption for all humanity. But our basic faith in the goodness of a higher power does not equip us with the academic wherewithal to construct a sophisticated explanation of the ultimate composition of human nature.

Yet as women we share a very profound experience that stands at the center of human existence: motherhood. At some point in our lives we have gone through the primal process of giving birth to another human being and nurturing our child to adulthood and beyond. One could say that mothers, in general, know better than anyone else what our most basic human instincts are all about. For this reason, we are

> **BOX 7.1**
> **JOSEFA DONATO DE PAUVI ON FAITH**
> I think there is something superior that gives us strength. I still believe
> in God. It is not very easy. I can't go into a church because I don't like
> the priests who govern the church. I can't go and confess with a priest
> because we feel they have been accomplices of the military, but inside
> me I feel there is a supreme being. Otherwise I would not be the way
> I am today.

puzzled to read in charge number 1 that instincts are reducible to self-preservation, competition, and violence. Clearly, this charge must have been formulated by men who, having never felt the depth and power of maternal instincts, made patriarchal violence the foundation of all human experience. Rest assured that most ordinary mothers do not agree with this strange idea that our most elemental instincts can be reduced to violent forms of self-preservation and competition. No doubt, selfishness and violence are part of the human experience, but to turn these sentiments into the basic components of human nature tells us more about the condition of the male psyche and its corresponding patriarchal social structures than it does about the true qualities of human nature and the actual characteristics of human instincts.

Just ask your own mothers and grandmothers if you don't believe us! Even during the intense pain of childbirth, women often have a keen sense of loving anticipation. And then, when you finally get to hold your newborn child in your arms, you are bathed in sentiments of love and tenderness for this tiny creature. Likewise, the baby craves the love of its mother with every fiber of its being. At such a moment, there is simply no room for selfishness or competitiveness. Moreover, to ascertain the inherent "sinfulness" of the human condition in this situation becomes but an exercise in abstract thinking. The truth is that maternal thinking is very different from abstract thinking. Sentiments of violence and self-preservation couldn't be any further from the mind of a mother caring for her newborn child. In fact, maternal instincts are so powerful that most mothers would easily sacrifice their own lives for the sake of their child.

Sure, there are the occasional exceptions to this rule. We have all heard of women who reject their infants, sometimes even going so far as to abandon or kill them. But if you look deeper than the sensational headlines in the newspapers, you usually find that these women did what they did as a result of a severe psychological disorder or immense social pressures. Once the initial shock wears off, these mothers tend to go through emotional agony as a consequence of their terrible actions. In general, however, mothers from many different cultural backgrounds can attest to the fact that the most basic instincts at the core of human existence are those of love, self-sacrifice, and care.

This is also the reason why we Mothers of the Plaza de Mayo adopted the *panuelo*, a white baby shawl, as one of the central symbols in our nonviolent struggle against the junta. Indeed, we often wear baby shawls as scarves or put them on banners during church services and in public squares as stark reminders of the regime's brutal interruption of our maternal tasks. The *panuelo* also signifies that the disappearance of our children has left us in a state of permanent pregnancy—a condition that gives us much strength to carry on our nonviolent revolution and makes us feel that our political engagement will eventually lead to the rebirth of Argentine society. Believe us, once you have witnessed hundreds of streamers made of baby shawls fluttering in the Plaza de Mayo during our weekly demonstrations, you'll understand that our struggle is not just about our own children but about the necessary task of

---

BOX 7.2
THE MOTHERS ON COLLECTIVE MATERNITY
The child of one is the child of all of us, not only those who are missing, but the ones who are fighting for their rights today. We learned this from our guts, not from philosophic concepts. . . . All children are ours. We teach them how to defend their rights, to demand them and exercise them. We feed them with love, wash them with the Plaza, love them by showing them a path toward struggle and liberty. We teach them that the struggle for life, justice, and liberty begins every morning when you wake up, open the curtains, and look at the sun.

extending love and care to all those people in the world, young and old, who suffer from the actions of a tyrannical regime.

Let us now turn to the second charge: *Nonviolence does not work in the real world. The proof of the impracticality of nonviolence is that its proponents do not achieve their desired political and social goals.*

Our nonviolent struggle had many goals. We wanted to find out what happened to our children. We wanted to prevent new disappearances. We wanted to bring down the military regime. We wanted to hold accountable all those persons responsible for the heinous crimes committed during the reign of the generals. We wanted to help family members to cope with their irreplaceable losses. We wanted to combat those extreme forms of militarism that pervade all Latin American societies. We wanted to transform the sexist cult of machismo and the overbearing culture of violence that socializes people into accepting lethal force as the most potent means of solving conflicts. Finally, we wanted to contribute to the noble effort of advancing social justice and human rights in all parts of the world.

We readily admit that our most pressing goal has always been to account for every single person who disappeared in Argentina during the horrendous years of the Dirty War. We have not reached this objective yet, partly because of the recalcitrance of the democratic governments that have succeeded the autocratic rule of the generals, and partly because much of the empirical evidence that could lead us to uncover the fates of our loved ones has been lost or destroyed. Because of that, we may never achieve our most immediate objective. But this is not the fault of the nonviolent method. Quite to the contrary, the nonviolent method has made it possible for us to achieve at least *some* of our goals.

For example, we brought down the junta without ever firing a shot. Language and the use of symbols became extremely important nonviolent weapons that managed to capture the public consciousness. We chose simple words with deeply emotional meanings to clarify political developments and to give presence not only to the disappeared but also to the heinous actions of the regime that were being swept under the rug. Slogans like "You must tell us where our children are," "They took them away alive, we want them returned alive," and "The junta will fall," expressed our emotions and political aspirations, and, like well-aimed nonviolent darts, unmasked the regime's terror. We continuously referred to the military as "assassins," "tortures," and "oppressors"—

BOX 7.3

MARIA DEL ROSARIO DE CERRUTI ON SPEAKING TRUTH TO POWER

One of the things that I simply will not do is shut up. The women of my generation in Latin America have been taught the man is always in charge and the woman is silent even in the face of injustice. We have to speak out about the injustices publicly. If not, we are accomplices. I am going to denounce them publicly without fear. This is what I have learned. This is the form the struggle takes.

---

terms that honestly characterized their despicable actions. Our insistence on naming the evil and speaking truth to power encouraged other citizens to do the same, thus making our movement even more effective.

Even when the generals unleashed their intimidating violence on us—mostly in the form of severe threats, beatings, arrests, or more disappearances—we refused to stop our weekly demonstrations on the Plaza de Mayo. We recruited more Mothers and traveled around the country to tell our story. We never ceased producing our underground newsletter. We kept writing our petitions to the generals even though we knew that they never read them. We continued establishing lasting connections to the international press and contacted important politicians abroad.

Some people say that the junta fell from power only because it lost the Falkland War against the British. Hence, they argue, it was more efficient forms of violence that put an end to the rule of the generals. That's just rubbish! We now know from the junta's own records that the tremendous pressure we exerted between 1977 and 1982 resulted in growing domestic problems that prompted the junta's last-ditch effort to divert public attention and whip up patriotic sentiments by embarking on this dramatic foreign-policy adventure. So while it is true that the humiliating battlefield defeat of the Argentine armed forces in June 1982 was the final straw that broke the regime's back, it must be emphasized that it was our nonviolent movement that prepared the way for our country's return to civilian government. When we opted for nonviolent resistance, many people thought we were just a bunch of crazy old women who didn't know anything about the power of violence. Our struggle proved the opposite: the violence of the generals proved to be

---

BOX 7.4

THE MOTHERS' DEMANDS TO ARGENTINA'S JUNTA

We don't judge our detained-disappeared children, nor do we ask for their freedom. We want to be told where they are, what they are accused of, and ask that they be judged according to the legal norms with the legitimate right of defense if they have committed any crimes. We ask that they not be tortured or kept in inhumane conditions and that we can see them and assist them.

---

no match for the nonviolence of mothers. In short, nonviolence actually does work in the real world of power politics.

Finally, allow us to briefly address the third charge: *Nonviolence does not provide adequate security. The refusal to employ defensive violence makes people far more vulnerable to their violent neighbors and enemies. To opt for nonviolence means to neglect one's social responsibility and risk the safety of one's community.*

What is there for us to say except that our own experience in Argentina is diametrically opposed to this charge? Our option for nonviolent resistance actually created a strong community where there was previously merely a collection of frightened individuals. Our nonviolent movement made our country more secure, both with regard to the domestic and foreign matters. It is our experience that military force—even when it is allegedly employed for "defensive purposes only"—tends to undermine the safety of the national community. In the Argentine case, for example, slogans such as "defending our country" and "protecting our national interests" were used to justify launching a full-scale attack against the British on the Falkland Islands. Surely, the exercise of military violence did not make Argentina a more secure place. What makes any community more secure is for its members to replace a system based on force by ties based on love. Once firmly established among community members, such ties cannot be broken even by the most violent enemy. "Community" is not merely a word referring to material relationships; it is also a term signifying an emotional and spiritual condition characterized by love and mutual aid.

Thus, dear jurors, having reflected on the three charges, we Mothers of the Plaza de Mayo have come to the conclusion that nonviolence should be found not guilty. It should be clear from our testimony that the assumptions contained in the three charges do not correspond to the realities of our struggle against one of the most brutal regimes of the twentieth century.

Questions for Cross-examination

1. Isn't the maternal instinct really about the self-preservation of the species as a whole? In that case, competition and violence are still inevitable in human affairs.
2. The Mothers argue that charge number 1 reduces all elemental instincts to violent forms of self-preservation and competition. By the some token are they reducing all elemental instincts to nonviolent forms of love and care?
3. How do the Mothers know that the maternal instinct is more central to human nature than other instincts?
4. Not all women are mothers, and, obviously, men are not subject to this instinct at all. How, then, can an instinct that affects less than 50 percent of humans be considered to be "standing at the center of the human existence"?
5. Even if it is true that the pressure exerted by the Mothers between 1977 and 1982 resulted in the junta's ill-advised military offensive against the Falkland Islands, did the regime gave up power only after it was defeated in a violent war?
6. Is it a form of psychological violence to call people "assassins," "torturers," and "oppressors"—even if they once engaged in despicable actions?
7. Do the Mothers fully address the third charge? After all, the core question of this charge is whether the refusal to employ defensive violence would make a community more vulnerable to their violent neighbors and enemies, that is, external aggressors.

Suggestions for Further Reading and Thinking

Topic 1. What Is Anarchism?

Some of the Mothers have referred to their movement as being rooted in anarchist principles. In the popular mind, anarchism is often associated with violence such as bombings and assassinations. This is unfortunate, because only a small fraction of anarchists support violent agitation. The vast majority of anarchists believe that nonviolent methods are much better suited to achieve their political goals. So what are their objectives?

According to Alexander Berkman (1870–1936), a prominent Russian anarchist, anarchism is a political ideology envisioning a society in which humans can live without compulsion of any kind. A life without compulsion naturally means liberty; it means freedom from being forced or coerced, a chance to lead the life that suits each person best. Most anarchists consider the state to be such a coercive structure; hence, they argue for the abolishment of the state in favor of small, decentralized communities.

In keeping with their political style, the Mothers's association with anarchism was more practical than theoretical. They rebelled against established societal norms and engaged in nonviolent direct action by which means they sought to transform Argentine society from below. They networked with outlawed union leaders to organize large-scale strikes against the junta. In good anarchist fashion, the Mothers supported the decentralization of power, thus focusing their criticism on coercive economic and political structures such as capitalism and the modern state.

Anarchist-inspired movements have recently made their appearances in the global demonstrations against corporate globalization. Defying established economic institutions such as the World Trade Organization and the International Monetary Fund, such groups are seeking to extend democracy through the creation of global forms of popular participation.

Do you think that nonviolent forms of anarchism are effective vehicles for social change? To learn more about anarchism, read Avrich's excellent study of prominent anarchists. To hear the Mothers's agenda in their own voices, watch the video *Las Madres* and familiarize yourself with Matilde Mellibovsky's very readable collection of their testimonies. Patricia Marchak's study provides the historical background and Jo Fisher offers an excellent overview of the Mothers's political agenda. Finally, an investigative journalist, Horacio Verbitsky, presents us with bone-chilling interviews with Francisco Scilingo, a retired Argentine navy officer who broke the military's code of silence and exposed the monstrous campaign of systematic torture and death waged by the junta from 1976 to 1982.

Suggested Reading

Paul Avrich. *Anarchist Portraits*. Princeton, N.J.: Princeton University Press, 1988.

Jo Fisher. *Mothers of the Disappeared*. Boston: South End Press, 1990.

Patricia Marchak. *God's Assassins: State Terrorism in Argentina in the 1970s*. Montreal: McGill–Queen's University Press, 1999.

Matilde Mellibovsky. *Circle of Love over Death: Testimonies of the Mothers of the Plaza de Mayo*. Willimantic, Conn.: Curbstone Press, 1997.

Horacio Verbitsky. *The Flight: Confessions of an Argentine Dirty Warrior*. New York: New Press, 1996.

Recommended Visual Materials

Las Madres: The Mothers of the Plaza de Mayo. Prod. and dir. Susana Munoz and Lourdes Portillo. Direct Cinema Ltd., 1985. Videocassette.

Useful Web Sites

www.madres.org

www.soaw.org/new

www.derechos.org/nizkor/arg/eng.html

Topic 2. Gender and Nonviolence: Revolutionary Motherhood

The study of the *Mothers of the Plaza de Mayo* and their nonviolent movement raises fascinating questions about the connection between gender and (non)violence. Are men more violent than women? Are women less drawn than men to hierarchical social structures, which tend to produce more violence than egalitarian ones? Would political institutions and systems dominated by women be less violent than our current structures? What do you think?

Certainly, the Mothers consciously referred to their maternal impulses as the source of energy behind their desired transformation of Argentina's militaristic and sexist society. They rejected the male model of abstract thinking and instead embraced passions and feelings as the source of their political empowerment. Arguing for continuity between the private and the public sphere, they celebrated a "new consciousness" that encouraged women to take control of their lives, expand the sphere of their activity, and move beyond society's constraints and gendered expectations. Seeing themselves as "revolutionary mothers," they encouraged other women to break through the barriers of male-dominated society and create new identities and spaces for themselves.

Both Marguerite Guzman Bouvard and Diana Taylor use the concept of "revolutionary motherhood" to discuss the significance of the Mothers's struggle not merely for Argentine politics but for feminist theory and practice in general. Finally, make sure to consult Sara Ruddick's fine study for an insightful discussion of how pregnancy and motherhood can be politicized to undermine the hypermasculine basis of militaristic thinking.

Suggested Reading

Marguerite Guzman Bouvard. *Revolutionizing Motherhood: The Mothers of the Plaza de Mayo.* Wilmington, Del.: Scholarly Resources, 1994.

Sara Ruddick. *Maternal Thinking: Toward a Politics of Peace.* Boston: Beacon Press, 1989.

Diana Taylor. *Disappearing Acts: Spectacles of Gender and Nationalism in Argentina's "Dirty War."* Durham, N.C.: Duke University Press, 1999.

Useful Web Sites

www.uoregon.edu/~audreylv/anarcha_biblio.htm
www.feminist.org

PART III

Considering Further Evidence

CHAPTER EIGHT

MODERN NONVIOLENCE MOVEMENTS

After listening to the testimonies of the expert witnesses, you, the jurors in this trial, are now being asked to consider further evidence introduced by the prosecution and the defense. The evidence presented in this chapter relates primarily to issues raised in the second and third charge dealing with the alleged impracticality of nonviolence and its inability to provide for adequate security arrangements.

Statement by the Prosecution

We wish to include in the record of these court proceedings further examples that clearly illustrate the necessity and effectiveness of violence. In fact, our expert witnesses have already pointed to a number of compelling examples. In particular, we would like the members of the jury to consider the following four cases: (1) the first wave of eighteenth-century social revolutions, which established democracy and the rule of law in France and the United States; (2) the second and third wave of democratic revolutions in the nineteenth and twentieth centuries, which occurred in different parts of the world; (3) the successful mobilization of Allied military and civilian forces against Nazi Germany and the empire of Japan in the twentieth century, which resulted in the creation of lasting democratic constitutions in those countries; (4) current international efforts coordinated by the United Nations to dispatch armed peacekeepers to various crisis regions in the world, as well as the formation of U.S.-led international alliances confronting rogue states like Iraq and Afghanistan that provide support to al-Qaeda and other global terrorist organizations.

Given the public's familiarity with these cases, the prosecution sees no compelling reason to present the jury with detailed descriptions of these events. We do, however, wish to reiterate that in our view these cases unmistakably point to the necessity and effectiveness of legitimate forms of violence in establishing democratic political systems and enhancing the security of the global community.

Statement by the Defense

We would like to present the jury with evidence drawn from modern nonviolent movements that are generally not known to large segments of the public. What follows, therefore, is a statement describing the success of these movements, which operated in various parts of the world. For reasons of fairness and equity, the presiding judge has asked us to keep our presentation as brief as possible, and by limiting it to four select cases we intend to comply with this request.

Before we introduce our cases, however, we would like to remind you that our expert witnesses have already exposed you to three major examples: Gandhi's *satyagraha* movements in South Africa and India, King's civil rights movement in the United States, and the Mothers of the

Plaza de Mayo's movement in Argentina. Seeking to assess the success or failure of Gandhi's and King's respective movements, a number of realist commentators have argued that the apparent achievements of these movements were due less to the nonviolent method than to the relatively "civilized" nature of the British and American governments and their "measured" response to nonviolent resisters. We would like to make three brief counterarguments.

First, civilized or not, the British and American governments operated in the "real world" of power politics, which constitutes the sole context for assessing the efficacy of nonviolence. Second, the reputation of these governments for being "civilized" and "measured" is often based on myth rather than historical fact. The truth is that they did not always act in a "civilized" way. As our example of Badshah Khan's nonviolent army in India's North-West Frontier Province will show, British imperialist forces acted with unimaginable cruelty against unarmed men, women, and children. The same can be said of a number of local, state, and federal governments in the United States, which, at least during the first half of the twentieth century, ignored or even encouraged brutal lynchings of black Americans and turned a blind eye to other vicious acts of racial violence committed by whites against other ethnic minorities. Third, as we have already seen in the Argentine case, various forms of nonviolent direct action appeared to be quite capable of securing at least some measure of success—even when employed against murderous regimes with absolutely no regard for human rights and the rule of law. Four additional cases presented in this chapter serve to substantiate this claim.

We begin our presentation with a brief account of nonviolent protests that took place in the heart of Berlin in 1943. No doubt, the Nazi dictatorship constitutes perhaps the toughest test imaginable for the nonviolent method because the former was the most inhumane regime of the twentieth century. Hence, the existence of effective nonviolent resistance to the Nazi dictatorship challenges the widespread belief that Gandhi's nonviolence movement could never work in Hitler's Germany. Sadly, only a few people know about these remarkable protests. This ignorance in turn strengthens the notion that nonviolence is incapable of challenging totalitarian regimes. After familiarizing yourself with the following cases, you'll be in a better position to judge the veracity of this assumption.

The Rosenstrasse Protests Against the Nazi Regime in Germany, 1943

In the winter of 1943, the Nazi regime was at the height of its power. Occupying most of Europe, Hitler's troops fought a crucial battle with the Russian Red Army in Stalingrad. The war against the Jews, too, was in full swing. At the secret 1942 Wannsee Conference, Nazi leaders had agreed to implement the Final Solution to the "Jewish problem" in the death camps of occupied Eastern Europe. In Berlin, the Gestapo and SS spearheaded this effort by arresting about 10,000 Jews in brutal night raids on February 27, 1943. Although many of these Jews had non-Jewish spouses, Nazi authorities did not hesitate to put most of them on cattle cars bound for the gas chambers of Auschwitz. A further 2,000 Jews who were awaiting transport to the same location were being held in a temporary collection center on a street called Rosenstrasse, in the heart of Berlin.

But the news of the mass arrests was spreading like wildfire through the city. Within a few hours, something happened that the regime had never counted on. A small number of the detained Jews' Gentile spouses—most of them women—established contact with each other and rushed to the Rosenstrasse collection center to protest the arrests of their loved ones. These women stood huddled together, adamantly demanding their husbands back. Several of them boldly approached the police and SS guards and complained angrily, insisting on their rights as German citizens. "If you don't let us in to see our spouses, we'll come back and make trouble," they barked at the baffled Nazi authorities. And back they came, accompanied by more relatives, friends, and sympathetic passersby. On the second day of the protests, about 150 people had gathered in an unprecedented demonstration of open German resistance to Nazi persecution of Jews. Walking up and down Rosenstrasse in tight groups with arms locked, the women chanted, "We want our husbands back!"

Day and night, for six days, these courageous women continued their protest, attracting ever-larger crowds until the street was crammed with people. Soon London radio stations began to draw its listeners' attention to the demonstration procession, calling it a significant show of resistance. The regime soon recovered from its initial shock and struck back. Under the supreme command of Joseph Goebbels, Hitler's propaganda minister and the party leader of Greater Berlin, the Gestapo forcibly removed the most vocal protesters and then proceeded to use heavy vehicles to disperse the crowds. Threatening to open fire on the protesters, the troops finally managed to clear the street—but only for a short while. Within an hour, most of the protesters returned and resumed their chants. Their presence made it impossible for the authorities to move the detainees to the concentration camp trains without being detected. By the sixth day of the protests, the crowd had swelled to more than a thousand angry demonstrators, including people who did not have imprisoned relatives. Slowly, the demonstrations began to assume a more obvious political, anti-Nazi tone as hundreds of voices rang out with screams of "Nazi murderers!"

The next day Goebbels gave orders for the immediate release of the detained Jews. He was clearly worried that the demonstrators would begin to organize a widespread resistance movement against the regime. As noted by Nathan Stoltzfus, the author of a meticulously researched book on the subject, the Nazi leaders were keenly aware that uncoerced popular accommodation, ranging from enthusiastic support to passive acceptance, was the primary basis of their political power. The nonviolent demonstrations threatened to undermine that consensual foundation, ultimately pressuring Goebbels to abandon the fundamental Nazi principle of racial purification for the crucial political imperative of avoiding domestic unrest. Thus, nonviolent direct action proved to be a potent weapon against the most lethal regime in the modern era. Imagine, dear jurors, what might have happened if millions of ordinary Germans had followed the example of the courageous Rosenstrasse protesters and stood up to Hitler's dictatorship!

The People Power Movement in the Philippines, 1985–86

In early 1986, Ferdinand Marcos had been ruling the Philippines with an iron fist for more than twenty years. Having declared martial law in 1972 for the alleged purpose of fighting "Communist rebels" more effectively, he and his wife, Imelda, exercised virtually unlimited dictatorial powers. Backed by the United States, the Marcos regime kept a watchful eye on any movement that might challenge its oppressive rule. Marcos's most powerful rival was Benigno Aquino, a former provincial governor and senator who had been imprisoned during the 1970s. In 1980, Aquino was allowed to travel to the United States for medical treatment. Accompanied by his wife, Cory, the former governor returned to his home country in 1983 and was promptly assassinated on leaving the plane. Although a civilian commission exposed a military conspiracy engineered behind the scenes by Ferdinand and Imelda Marcos, the country's high court ignored the commission's findings and acquitted the implicated military officers in 1985.

Unsettled by a broad, popular-based opposition movement that had become very active after the murder of Aquino, Marcos attempted to legitimize his political rule by calling for an open presidential election in February 1986. After all, he knew how to manipulate elections. During a parliamentary election two years earlier, his regime had committed massive fraud, including the stuffing of ballot boxes. This time, however, many ordinary Filipinos, vowing to keep a watchful eye on the proceedings, organized sustained nonviolent protests such as marches, rallies, and group jogging in order to avoid a repetition of the 1984 election fraud. Cory Aquino ran for president as the "people's candidate," and early election returns indicated a decisive victory. Before the final vote was announced, the regime once again manipulated the vote tallies in order to thwart Aquino's triumph at the polls. Outraged, the people took to the streets by the hundreds of thousands.

Much to their credit, the protesters followed Aquino's orders to employ only nonviolent methods such as demonstrations, mass strikes, refusal to pay utility bills, selective consumer boycotts, refusal to send children to school, and the withdrawal of funds from banks controlled by Marcos's cronies. Soon known as People Power, the nonviolent movement increasingly drew support from members of the Catholic church hierarchy, the business elite, and a small fraction of the armed forces. Its millions of rural, working-class, middle-class, and professional supporters were united by their Catholic faith and their conviction that the Marcos regime had to go. For eighteen days, millions of demonstrators refused to leave the streets of Manila, singing and praying for the deliverance of their nation from tyranny. Marcos promptly ordered the military to disperse the crowds by any means necessary. But the dispatched tanks and armored personnel carriers were immediately surrounded by thousands of people who met the troops with kind words, gifts, and flowers. When low-flying helicopters appeared with guns pointed at the crowds, the people stood their ground and sang "Ave Maria."

Deeply affected by these honest expressions of goodwill and nonviolent faith, the soldiers loyal to Marcos refused to open fire. As the demonstrations wore on, they defected in increasing numbers, risking certain court-martial if Marcos prevailed. However, when the Catholic Bishops Conference of the Philippines formally endorsed active resistance against the Marcos regime and called on people to continue their "nonviolent struggle for justice," two key military leaders—Defense Minister Juan Ponce Enrile and Lt. General Fidel Ramos—announced their decision to support People Power. Watching incredulously how nonviolent direct action had prompted a full-scale revolt of the armed forces, the Marcos family caved in and fled the country, paving the way for the establishment of a democratic government headed by President Cory Aquino. Ironically, President Ronald Reagan granted Marcos and his entourage political asylum in Honolulu, Hawai'i, and thus sheltered the dictator from legal prosecution.

It seems that the Filipino people never forgot the effectiveness of the nonviolent method. In January 2001, thousands of nonviolent demonstrators hit the streets calling for the ouster of President Joseph Estrada—a man accused of bribery, graft, and corruption; betrayal of public trust; and violation of the constitution. As a result of these mass protests, eleven cabinet secretaries resigned their posts and the government collapsed. Encouraged by the broad range of civil society groups that campaigned for Estrada's removal, police and military officials soon withdrew their support from the corrupt president. The Supreme Court then declared the presidency vacant, and Vice President Gloria Macapagal-Arroyo was sworn in as president. Fifteen years after the Marcos ouster, nonviolent People Power had once again triumphed in the Philippines.

The Nonviolent Velvet Revolution in Czechoslovakia, 1989

In the late 1980s, the political situation in Communist Eastern Europe was slowly changing. Having introduced *glasnost* ("openness") and *perestroika* ("economic restructuring")—two initiatives aimed at reforming Communism from within—the dynamic Soviet leader Mikhail Gorbachev let it be known that the Soviet Union would no longer interfere with the "internal affairs" of its satellite states. This announcement constituted a remarkable change in policy, given that the Soviet Union had previously dispatched thousands of troops to suppress popular revolts against the Communist regimes of East Germany, Hungary, Poland, and Czechoslovakia.

The Soviet intervention in Czechoslovakia had been a particularly dramatic event. During the Prague Spring of 1968, the Czech Communist party leader, Alexander Dubček, announced the creation of a "socialism with a human face," which allowed citizens greater political and economic liberties. A few months later, his short period of openness came to a brutal end when Warsaw Pact forces led by the Soviet Union invaded Czechoslovakia. Dubček was replaced by Gustav Husak, a bland party bureaucrat chosen by Moscow to engineer his country's return to Communist "normalcy." During the 1970s, Husak mercilessly persecuted and jailed Vaclav Havel, Jiri Hajek, and other leaders of Charter 77, a small human rights group that had formed in opposition to the Communist regime.

Ten years later, new anticommunist resistance movements in Czechoslovakia and other Eastern European countries emerged, partly because of Gorbachev's new course and partly because of the success of a popular nonviolence movement in Poland. Under the capable leadership of the Gdansk shipyard worker Lech Walesa, Polish workers had formed their own free trade union called Solidarity. Supported by millions of ordinary Poles, including high-ranking members of the Catholic church, Solidarity challenged the Communist Party's monopoly on political power by organizing mass demonstrations, general strikes, crippling boycotts, and other forms of nonviolent direct action. Government attempts to violently repress the movement failed. Desperately clinging to their posts, the Communist leaders finally agreed to recognize Solidarity and allow free parliamentary elections. In June 1989, the Communist Party was trounced at the polls and forced to cede power to a Solidarity-led coalition government. The first bloodless transition from Communism to democracy during this remarkable year set the signal for other countries. On November 9, citizens of East and West Berlin jointly dismantled the infamous Berlin Wall without firing a single shot.

In Czechoslovakia, the so-called Velvet Revolution against the Communist regime started on November 17, 1989, in Prague, when students held a nonviolent mass demonstration to demand democratic reforms. Riot police viciously beat hundreds of these nonviolent marchers. But their attempts to disperse the crowd failed as students refused to clear the streets. Unwilling to respond to the regime's brutality in kind, some students even offered flowers to the police. The next day, several labor union leaders declared their solidarity with the stu-

Figure 8.1 Nonviolent Protesters in Prague, November 1989. Courtesy of Corbis.

dents and organized mass demonstrations in major cities. The protesters skillfully employed nonviolent tactics such as street theater and public discussions. As a result of these conversations, the demonstrators spontaneously formed Civic Forum and The Public Against Violence, two new organizations that represented their common interests.

As the nonviolent mass demonstrations grew in size and intensity, the Communist leadership sought to give the appearance that it was willing to become more responsive to the calls for democratic reforms. Some hardliners were forced to resign and a relatively unknown party bureaucrat was elected as the new party leader. But the public was not duped by these maneuvers. In fact, nearly half a million protesters gathered at the Letna football stadium for one of the largest political rallies ever held in Czechoslovakia. On November 27, the opposition staged a successful general strike. Hundreds of thousands of ordinary citizens gathered at Wenceslas Square in Prague and jangled their keys as a symbolic gesture signifying the unlocking of their political prison. For hours, protesters just stood still, their keys producing the sound of freedom that effectively ended four decades of authoritarian rule. A few days later, the Communist regime capitulated and agreed to a list of sweeping democratic demands presented by Vaclav Havel, the leader of Civic Forum. On December 10, a new government took the reigns of power and Havel was elected president of Czechoslovakia. Free local and parliamentary elections held in 1990 brought the nonviolent Velvet Revolution to a successful end.

There is no doubt, dear jurors, that nonviolent social movements were a highly significant factor in the demise of Communist regimes in Eastern Europe. Mobilizing large crowds, the leaders of these movements devised creative and thought-provoking tactics to communicate their vision. With the exception of Romania, where some violence was used to overthrow the Ceausescu regime, these movements engaged in nonviolent direct action to exert pressure on the communist leadership. As pointed out by the social-movement scholar Lester R. Kurtz in *Nonviolent Social Movements*, nonviolence was largely successful as a function of the *paradox of repression*. This paradox holds that in a conflict involving asymmetrical power relations—when the more powerful oppressor exercises violence to destroy its nonviolent challenger—violent repression ironically weakens the regime's authority and strengthens the nonviolent opposition. Paradoxically, the more the regime exercises violence to hold on to power, the more citizens and third parties are likely to become disaffected, sometimes to such an extreme that the regime disintegrates rapidly. The Velvet Revolution is an example of this paradox of repression, demonstrating the effectiveness of nonviolence and its applicability in the real world of power politics.

Badshah Khan's Nonviolent Army in Northwest India, 1930s

Western commentators with a scant understanding of Islam frequently allege that Muslim societies are unremittingly violent and incapable of sustaining nonviolent movements. In addition to demonizing the Muslim "other," this dangerous myth serves to downplay the achievements of Islamic civilizations. In fact, one of the largest and best-organized social movements based on Gandhi's principles of *satyagraha* emerged in the 1930s in the mountainous border region of modern-day Pakistan and Afghanistan. The leader of this remarkable movement was a charismatic Pashtun chief and devout Muslim who challenged the oppressive colonial rule of the British with an army of 100,000 nonviolent "Servants of God."

Known as Badshah Khan ("king of tribal chiefs"), Abdul Ghaffar Khan was born in 1889 in Utmanzai, a small village located in the sprawling Peshawar valley of India's North-West Frontier Province. Although this region had been under indirect British colonial rule for decades, the Europeans faced periodic revolts staged by indigenous Pashtun tribes. In 1842, for example, these fierce Islamic mountain warriors wiped out a British army of 4,500 men. In response, the British sent scores of punitive expeditions into the treacherous terrain. These troops shelled the Pashtun strongholds, burned their mountain villages, and destroyed their harvests. Determined to "teach these savages a lesson," the British flogged, killed, and jailed thousands. But rather than breaking Pashtun resistance, these reprisals only provoked further counterattacks. As a result of their indomitable will to resist their colonial masters, the Pashtuns acquired among the British the reputation of being the world's most fearless and violent people, bound together by ancient warrior codes and interested only in the art of killing.

Badshah Khan was the son of a prominent village chief and grew up watching this endless cycle of colonial repression and Pashtun rebellion. For the boy the lesson was obvious: violence had failed to accomplish the "pacification" of the North-West Frontier Province. Deeply impressed by Mahatma Gandhi's method of *satyagraha*, Khan traveled to remote Pashtun hamlets to open schools and improve the social conditions of the villagers. British authorities told him repeatedly that his educational efforts were not welcome because he "made the villagers think." Disregarding their warnings and constant threats, Khan continued his work. Arrested on trumped-up charges, he spent several years in prison. Upon release, the undeterred social reformer decided to mount a comprehensive nonviolent challenge to British rule in the North-West Frontier Province. First, he started *Pushtun*, a native-language journal carrying articles on political and social issues as well as on Islamic law. For the Pashtun leader, Islam was a religion of love and nonviolence dedicated to the full realization of social and political equality, including race and gender equality. The journal was an instant success and carried Khan's nonviolent message to a mass audience.

Second, in 1929, Khan began to organize history's first professional nonviolent army. Any Pashtun could join, provided he took the army's oath of serving humanity in the name of Allah, refraining from violence and taking revenge, and living a simple life dedicated to social reform. Calling

Figure 8.2
Badshah
Khan,
1889–
1988.
Courtesy
of Corbis.

themselves *Khudai Khitmatgars*, or Servants of God, the volunteers formed
platoons with commanding officers and learned basic army discipline.
They had drills, badges, a tricolor flag, and even a bagpipe corps and wore
red uniforms—everything that did not require the use of arms. Within a
few years, Khan's organization grew from a small group of a few dozen to
an army of nearly 100,000 soldiers. Following Gandhi's call for resistance
against the British, the Servants of God engaged in civil disobedience and
other forms of nonviolent direct action against the colonizers. In what
could hardly be called a "civilized response," the British harassed, beat, and
killed scores of unarmed resisters. Moreover, they confiscated private property and sacked entire villages to recover fines. Stunned by the Pashtun's
commitment to remain nonviolent even in the face of such atrocities, the
European colonizers raised the level of repression, hoping to provoke violent responses. On April 23, 1930, British troops opened fire on unarmed
crowds at the Quissa Khawani Bazaar, killing more than two hundred nonviolent demonstrators. Khan was arrested and spent most of the decade in
prison. Braving the miserable conditions in jail as well as the cruel treatment of the prison guards, Khan was gratified to hear that his Servants of
God were adhering to their oath of nonviolence and continuing their civil
disobedience campaign in his absence.

In 1938, Gandhi toured the North-West Frontier Providence
together with Badshah Khan who had only recently been released from

prison. Deeply touched by the commitment to nonviolence shown by the Servants of God, Gandhi acknowledged their crucial role in India's struggle for independence. Like their leader, these Pashtun warriors were not born nonviolent but had had to completely remake themselves. They proved that even people steeped in violent traditions could practice nonviolence in a politically effective way. Moreover, Badshah Khan's Servants of God showed to the world that the highest religious values of Islam were clearly compatible with a deep commitment to nonviolence.

Dear jurors, these four cases are but select examples of the much larger modern nonviolence movement. Other cases include the nonviolent resistance movement to the Nazi occupation in Denmark, Norway, and Holland (1940s); Cesar Chavez's farmworkers' movement in the United States (1950s to 1970s); the consumer-boycott movement against apartheid in South Africa (1980s); the first *intifada* in occupied Palestine (late 1980s); the Ogoni struggle for human rights in Nigeria (1990s); the Serbian "Otpor!" movement that brought down the dictator Slobodan Milosevic (1998 to 2000); the pro-democracy movement in Burma led by a winner of the Nobel Peace Prize, Aung San Suu Kyi (ongoing); and the worldwide anti–corporate globalization movements (ongoing). All these cases demonstrate that recent social movements have successfully employed nonviolence in struggles against systems of political repression.

While no case is completely pure and clear, they all illustrate what the peace researcher Johan Galtung, in *Peace by Peaceful Means*, calls the three basic concerns of nonviolent action: (1) nonviolent action is directed against the relation of Self and Other, not against the Other as such; (2) nonviolent action is carried out in such a way as to build peaceful rather than violent behavior; and (3) the objective is not the annihilation of the opponent but its transformation and integration in a future society. Of course, nonviolent movements do not always achieve their goals. But, dear jurors, they are more successful than the prosecution team would care to admit.

Suggested Reading

Peter Ackerman and Jack Duvall. *A Force More Powerful: A Century of Nonviolent Conflict*. New York: St. Martin's Press, 2000.

Johan Galtung. *Peace by Peaceful Means*. London: Sage Publications, 1996.

Jack Goldstone, ed. *Revolutions: Theoretical, Comparative, and Historical Studies*. 3rd ed. Wadsworth, 2002.

John Hillen. *Blue Helmets: The Strategy of UN Military Operations*. Dulles, Va.: Brassey's, 2000.

Mary Kaldor. *New and Old Wars: Organized Violence in a Global Era*. Palo Alto, Calif.: Stanford University Press, 1999.

Michael Ledeen. *The War Against the Terror Masters*. New York: St. Martin's Press, 2002.

Rahul Mahajan. *The New Crusade: America's War on Terrorism*. New York: Monthly Review Press, 2002.

Kenneth M. Pollack. *The Threatening Storm: The Case for Invading Iraq*. New York: Random House, 2002.

Milan Rai. *Ten Reasons Against War with Iraq*. London: Verso, 2002.

Nathan Stoltzfus. *Resistance of the Heart: Intermarriage and the Rosenstrasse Protest*. New York: W. W. Norton, 1996.

Stephen Zunes, Lester R. Kurtz, and Sara Beth Asher, eds. *Nonviolent Social Movements: A Geographical Perspective*. Malden, Mass.: Blackwell, 1999.

Recommended Visual Materials

A Force More Powerful: A Century of Nonviolent Conflict. Written by, prod., and dir. Steve York. 2000. Broadcast on PBS and WETA. Available on videocassette.

Bringing Down a Dictator. Written by, prod., and dir. Steve York. 2001. Broadcast on PBS and WETA. Available on videocassette.

Useful Web Sites

www.chambon.org/rosenstrasse.htm
www.topographie.de/en/rosen.htm
www.aforcemorepowerful.org
www.biblio-india.com/articles/jf02_ar5.asp?mp=JF02

CHAPTER NINE

SCIENTIFIC EVIDENCE ON HUMAN VIOLENCE
Nature or Nurture?

Statement by the Prosecution

Statement by the Defense

Arriving at a Verdict

Suggested Reading

Before you are asked to withdraw for your final deliberations, please consider further empirical evidence related to the question of "human nature" raised in the first charge. The prosecution and the defense have prepared short statements that enlist influential scientific theories of human aggression to probe the extent to which human beings actually possess the biological and social equipment to conduct their affairs non-violently. Your task is to read through these statements carefully and weigh the conflicting scientific evidence. Is violence part of our biological makeup or is it the result of specific social arrangements? You are encouraged to delve further into this longstanding nature/nurture debate on violence by consulting the books listed at the end of this chapter.

Statement by the Prosecution

The core idea of our statement is simple and straightforward: there exists plenty of scientific evidence for our claim that violence and aggression are rooted in human nature. Contemporary biological-instinctual theories of aggression do not simply echo outdated nineteenth-century ideas that violence is the result of simple genetic transmission from parent to child. We emphatically acknowledge that various social and cultural factors can influence the level of violence in society, but we resolutely reject the notion that violence and aggression are entirely the result of the social environment. Because humans are naturally endowed with an instinct of aggression, it is this innate drive that, in the last instance, accounts for individual and group violence in society. Indeed, members of all known human societies have, at one time or another, engaged in violent behavior. We challenge the defense to offer credible scientific evidence for the existence of totally nonviolent societies. We do not know of any such evidence. Short of changing our human nature, the idea of creating a nonviolent society will forever remain the unrealizable dream of naïve idealists.

Please allow us to substantiate our claims by making reference to some relevant insights drawn from biological-instinctual theories. The Austrian behavioral scientist Konrad Lorenz has assembled the most comprehensive evidence for the existence of aggressive instincts in animals and humans. Known as the father of modern ethology—the study of animals in their natural environment—Lorenz shared with two others the 1973 Nobel Prize for Physiology or Medicine for their path-breaking research on animal behavior. In his highly accessible book *On Aggression*, Lorenz presents his readers with the fruits of his scientific research on the subject of violence. His theory of aggression is firmly anchored in Darwinian evolutionary science. His observations confirm the existence of genetic links between animals and humans, a biological fact that is reflected in striking parallels between human and animal behavior. These behavioral parallels, Lorenz claims, show beyond doubt that genetic factors fuel aggressive human behavior, including warfare and other collective forms of violence. Drawing on his extensive work with animals, Lorenz concludes that innate violent instincts might not only be triggered by certain situations, such as the defense of territory, but could also spontaneously discharge without any external stimulation. According to Lorenz, the innate aggressive drive in animal and humans serves a number of vital purposes, including the economical spacing of various species in large habitats, mate selection, the defense of the young, and the formation of a hierarchical "pecking order" providing leadership and stability beneficial for the entire group. Violent drives, Lorenz admits, are a double-edged sword: they can pose serious dangers, but they also are necessary to preserve the species. Without an innate aggression drive, most species would be condemned to early extinction.

Lorenz's theory of innate aggression has been corroborated by a large number of leading scientists working in many fields, including the prominent ethologist Desmond Morris who laid out his ideas in *The Naked Ape*. The anthropologist Robert Ardrey, in *The Territorial Imperative*, has linked human aggressive behavior to an innate instinct to acquire and defend territory by violent means. Refining Sigmund Freud's theory of instinctual aggression, many psychoanalysts have studied the destructive potential of the "death instinct" in humans. Arguing that humans are genetically programmed to be violent, the sociobiologist and Pulitzer Prize–winning author E. O. Wilson advances his thesis that all social behavior rests on a biological foundation. Moreover, scores of medical research on identical twins and adopted children listed in Elizabeth Kandel Englander's *Understanding Violence* suggests a strong genetic basis for aggressive behavior.

BOX 9.1
LORENZ ON THE "AGGRESSION DRIVE"
Knowledge of the fact that the aggression drive is a true, primarily species-preserving instinct enables us to recognize its full danger: it is the spontaneity of the instinct that makes it so dangerous. If it were merely a reaction to certain external factors, as many sociologists and psychologists maintain, the state of mankind would not be as perilous as it really is, for, in that case, the reaction-eliciting factors could be eliminated with some hope of success. . . . The fact that the central nervous system does not need to wait for stimuli, like an electric bell with a push-button, before it can respond, but can itself produce stimuli which give a natural, physiological explanation for "spontaneous" behavior of animals and humans, has found recognition only in the last decades.

Let us emphasize again that scientists favoring a biological-instinctual approach readily acknowledge that biology is not the only factor responsible for violent human behavior. No doubt, culture and social conditioning continuously shape our instinctual violence. However, the external manipulation of our social environment can never entirely eliminate our aggression drive, because violence is a constantly building energy that demands discharge. Even if we were somehow capable of withholding all aggression-eliciting environmental stimuli from people, we would nonetheless fail to deactivate fully our aggression drive. In fact, as Konrad Lorenz has pointed out, attempts to artificially block the discharge of human aggression actually strengthen people's suicidal tendencies as they are forced to turn their innate violent impulses against themselves.

But what if biological-instinctual theories could be proved wrong? What if the innate aggression drive simply does not exist? We have two responses to these purely hypothetical objections. First, the fact that nobody has conclusively disproved the existence of such instincts speaks for itself. We leave it to you to draw the appropriate conclusion. Second, even if biological-instinctual theories of aggression could be proved wrong, this does not necessarily mean that violence could be completely eliminated from the human condition. For example, the Yale psychologist John Dollard and his colleagues in *Frustration and Aggression* put forth a social theory of aggression based on the hypothesis that violent behavior results from frustration. In other words, when people are blocked from meeting their basic needs or reaching their desired goals, they become irritable and aggressive. Given that members of all human societies have always experienced such moments of frustration, violence will always remain part of the human condition. Although we strongly support a biological-instinctual approach, one does not necessarily have to agree with such theories of aggression to accept the inevitability of violence—particularly in politics and other modes of social interaction characterized by conflict, goal orientation, and frustration.

In conclusion, let us return to a critical point made at the beginning of this statement. If nonviolence is indeed a real human possibility, why hasn't it been realized in *some* society, past or present? Of course, we do know of societies and tribes characterized by a remarkably low level of individual and collective violence. This seems to confirm the important role of culture and social conditioning as potentially moderating or exacerbating influences on human aggression. We have already conceded this point. By the same token, however, it should be noted that the absence of completely nonviolent societies points to sources of human violence that reach much deeper than fleeting social and cultural arrangements. Supported by a mountain of scientific evidence, our contention is this: the deep sources of violence are to be found in the very fabric of human nature. Hence, violence is inevitable in human affairs, particularly in power politics.

Statement by the Defense

We consider it a serious mistake to assume that humans have some fixed biological nature or an innate aggression drive that makes them violent. Contrary to the assertions of the prosecution, we maintain that the deepest sources of human violence and aggression are to be found in culture and the social environment. As our scientific evidence will show, people have the capability of learning to behave in many different ways, depending on the incentives and feedback provided by their ecological and social environment. Violence is not an inevitable feature of human nature but a learned behavior that can be changed. Thus, the idea of humanity remaining forever confined to violent societies is but a dangerous myth of pessimistic "realists." Please allow us to substantiate our claims by making reference to some relevant insights drawn from social learning theories.

The prosecution has referred to Konrad Lorenz, Sigmund Freud, and a whole slew of prominent scientists who subscribe to biological-instinctual theories of aggression. However, the prosecution has failed to inform you that there are scores of equally prominent scientists who strongly disagree with these theories on the basis of conflicting evidence obtained through scientific observation and experimentation. In 1986, in the Spanish city of Seville, a group of such prominent international scientists working in the fields of psychology, ethology, medicine, neurophysiology, anthropology, education, sociology, psychiatry, psychobiology, biochemistry, and political science issued a joint statement on violence. Condemning the misuse of scientific theories and data to naturalize violence and war, these scientists stated their position in the form of five propositions.

The scientists concluded their statement with an emphatic rejection of the prosecution's thesis that our biology condemns us to perpetual aggression and violence. The reason why so many people accept the false idea that there exists an instinctive cause for human aggression is their *social*

BOX 9.2
EXCERPTS FROM THE 1986 SEVILLE STATEMENT
ON VIOLENCE

1. It is scientifically incorrect to say that humans inherited a tendency to engage in violent acts and make wars from our animal ancestors. Warfare is a peculiarly human phenomenon and does not occur in other animals. . . .

2. It is scientifically incorrect to say that war or any other violent behavior is genetically programmed into our human nature. While genes are involved at all levels of nervous system function, they provide a developmental potential that can be actualized only in conjunction with the ecological and social environment. . . .

3. It is scientifically incorrect to say that in the course of human evolution there has been a selection for aggressive behavior more than for other kinds of behavior. Violence is neither in our evolutionary legacy nor is it in our genes. . . .

4. It is scientifically incorrect to say that humans have a "violent brain." While we do have the neural apparatus to act violently, it is not automatically activated by internal or external stimuli. There is nothing in our neurophysiology that compels us to react violently. . . .

5. It is scientifically incorrect to say that war is caused by "instinct" or any single motivation. . . .

experience of individual and collective acts of violence, including devastating global wars and horrendous genocides. Unfortunately, the obvious complexity of the social forces responsible for creating this culture of violence is eagerly exchanged for the apparent simplicity of the biological "answer." Many people simply do not realize that a great number of scientists have discarded the notion of "instincts" altogether. For example, Ashley Montagu, a celebrated anthropologist and social biologist, has noted that the concept of "instinct" represents the outstanding example of reification in the whole realm of science, that is, the employment of an abstraction as if it had real existence. The revival of this abstraction by Lorenz and others has been thoroughly rejected by many scientists who object to the use of the term "instinct" on strong grounds of evidence and theory. In short, the idea of an innate aggressive drive does not belong in the rational domain of science but in the misty realm of myth.

Many scientists have been searching for "violence genes" for decades, but they have not been able to find it. What can we conclude from that? Perhaps we ought to listen to leading researchers who emphasize that there simply exists no consistent evidence for a genetic basis for aggression, antisocial behavior, delinquency, criminality, and other forms of violence. Study after study has shown how people's behavior and attitudes can be modified by social conditioning and education. In fact, the pioneering work of the ethologist Frans de Waal with African chimpanzees, described in *Peacemaking Among Primates*, suggests that even animals do not possess an innate aggression drive. Decades ago, the psychologist Loh Tseng Tsai demonstrated that a rat-killing cat and a sewer rat can be taught by a combination of operant conditioning and social learning to eat peacefully out of the same dish. In his pathbreaking comparative studies of aggression in animals and humans, the German ethologist Irenaus Eibl-Eibesfeldt found no biological basis for postulating an innate imperative to kill. Such scientific discoveries have successfully challenged the traditional dogma of some psychologists that in animal nature there exists an ineradicable instinct of aggression that makes wars and other forms of collective violence inevitable.

Let's face it: the old idea that genetics determines our behavior is clearly mistaken; all human behavior is learned. Social learning theories of aggression correctly emphasize that people's violent behavior is the

---

BOX 9.3

ASHLEY MONTAGU ON THE MYTH OF INNATE VIOLENCE

The myth of early man's aggressiveness belongs in the same class as the myth of "the beast," that is, the belief that most if not all "wild" animals are ferocious killers. In the same class belong the myth of "the jungle," "the wild," "the warfare of Nature," and, of course, the myth of "innate depravity" or "original sin." These myths represent the projection of our acquired deplorabilities upon the screen of "nature." What we are unwilling to acknowledge as essentially our own making, we saddle upon "Nature," upon "phylogenetically programmed" or "innate" factors.

result of what has been learned from experience by observing and imitating the behavior of other members of society. Of course, we are not denying that humans possess the biological capacity to engage in violent behavior. Even if, for the sake of the argument, we granted that genetics predisposes people to aggression, this does not mean that violence is determined by our genes. Biological predispositions can be neutralized or even reversed by social conditioning.

Finally, please allow us to respond directly to the prosecution's challenge to offer some credible scientific evidence for the existence of nonviolent societies. Of course, there is such evidence. We are baffled by the prosecution's apparent ignorance of the vast scientific literature on this subject. For example, Ashley Montagu and other anthropologists have long documented the existence of nonaggressive societies like the Arapesh of New Guinea, the Semai of Malaya, and Hopi of North America, as described in Montagu's *Learning Non-Aggression*. This demonstrates that, at least within the framework of small societies, nonviolent principles are capable of guiding human interaction.

The Buid of the Philippines represent one of the most striking examples of how humans can solve their problems and conflicts without engaging in violent behavior. After spending considerable time with members of this little-known tribe residing deep in the jungles of the island of Mindoro, the anthropologist Thomas Gibson, in *Sacrifice and Sharing in the Philippine Highlands*, reported that the social affairs of the Buid are conducted on the basis of nonviolent strategies such as conflict avoidance and ignoring, negotiation, mediation, arbitration, and adjudication. Considering violence a form of insanity, the Buid have thus constructed elaborate social rules of nonviolent conflict resolution. For example, the Buid look very favorably upon a person who runs away from an outside aggressor. In their view, such honorable behavior deserves public recognition.

Gibson has identified several factors he considers crucial for an adequate explanation of Buid nonviolence. First, the Buid cultivate fluid family patterns; marriages and divorces occur frequently. Gibson estimates that the average Buid man or woman has five to ten significant partners in his or her lifetime. Second, the Buid have developed strong negative associations with violence in the past as they were subject to frequent raids by violent people from other islands. Since then, they have lived in relative isolation, avoiding contact with outsiders. Gibson speculates that the avoidance and nonviolent resolution of conflict became synonymous with survival and thus assumed a strong value in Buid society. Third, the Buid are bound together by extremely strong egalitarian social structures characterized by an emphasis on sharing and the avoidance of accumulated wealth.

Anthropological research into nonviolent societies such as that of the Buid bears out the insights gleaned from social learning theories of aggression. Every human being has the biological capacity for violence *and* nonviolence; people are not "naturally" one way or the other. Depending on our culture and social environment, we all learn to engage in different sorts of behavior. To assume that our biological potential for violence will always be expressed in terms of cultural values is scientifically wrong. Moreover, such facile generalizations are dangerous, self-fulfilling prophecies. Unless we humans are willing to accept the very real possibility of our planet's destruction as the result of our learned aggressive behavior, we must develop the courage to break the cycle of violence. The scientific evidence marshaled in this statement shows that it can be done. Thus, our contention is this: violence can be avoided in human affairs, even in power politics.

Arriving at a Verdict

Dear jurors, the time has come for you to withdraw to your room and deliberate. Please review the "instructions to the jurors" in chapter 1. Most of all, bear in mind that you have been asked to make a sincere commitment to consider the facts in an impartial and unbiased manner in order to uncover the truth. For this reason, you might want to find a few minutes of quiet time to reflect on the witnesses' testimonies and other evidence presented to you in this trial. Feel free to go back to specific chapters and arguments and refresh your memory. You may also want to reconsider some questions for cross-examination.

The fate of nonviolence is now in your hands. You may find it guilty or not guilty on all or specific counts. Regardless of how you judge nonviolence, be aware of the significance of your verdict. If you find the defendant guilty on all three counts, then at least the reasons for your decision are now much clearer to you. In addition, you are now familiar with the main arguments of both sides. If, on the other hand, you find nonviolence not guilty on one or more counts, then it is morally incumbent upon all of us to initiate the kinds of changes that are likely to make this world a less violent place. Deliberate carefully.

Suggested Reading

Robert Ardrey. *The Territorial Imperative: A Personal Inquiry into the Animal Origins of Property and Nations.* New York: Atheneum, 1966.

John Dollard et. al. *Frustration and Aggression.* New Haven: Yale University Press, 1939.

Elizabeth Kandel Englander. *Understanding Violence.* 2nd ed. Mahwah, N.J.: Lawrence Erlbaum Associates, 2003.

Richard I. Evans, ed. *Konrad Lorenz: The Man and His Ideas.* New York: Harcourt Brace Jovanovich, 1975.

Sigmund Freud. *Civilization and Its Discontents.* New York: W. W. Norton, 1930.

Thomas Gibson. *Sacrifice and Sharing in the Philippine Highlands: Religion and Society Among the Buid of Mindoro.* London: Athlone Press, 1986.

Konrad Lorenz. *On Aggression.* New York: Harcourt, Brace & World, 1966.

Ashley Montagu, ed. *Man and Aggression.* 2nd ed. New York: Oxford University Press, 1973.

Ashley Montagu, ed. *Learning Non-Aggression: The Experience of Non-Literate Societies.* New York: Oxford University Press, 1978.

Desmond Morris. *The Naked Ape: A Zoologist's Study of the Human Animal.* New York: McGraw-Hill, 1967.

Glenn D. Paige. *Nonkilling Global Political Science.* Honolulu: Center for Global Nonviolence, 2002.

Frans de Waal. *Peacemaking Among Primates.* Cambridge, Mass.: Harvard University Press, 1989.

E. O. Wilson. *Sociobiology: The New Synthesis.* Cambridge, Mass.: Harvard University Press, 1975.

Useful Web Sites

www.unesco.org/cpp/uk/declarations/seville.pdf
www.psy.pdx.edu/PsiCafe/KeyTheorists/Lorenz.htm
www.montagu.org
dmoz.org/Science/Biology/Sociobiology

INDEX

('b' indicates boxed material)